HOMICIDE in FAMILIES

And Other Special Populations

Ann Goetting, PhD, is Professor of Sociology at Western Kentucky University. Her broad and diverse publication record concentrates on the sociology of the family and criminology. With Sarah Fenstermaker, she co-edited *Individual Voices, Collective Visions: Fifty Years of Women in Sociology* (Temple University Press, 1995).

HOMICIDE
in FAMILIES

And Other Special Populations

ANN GOETTING, PhD

SPRINGER PUBLISHING COMPANY

Springer Publishing Company, Inc.
536 Broadway
New York, NY 10012-3955

Cover design by Tom Yabut
Production Editor: Pam Ritzer

95 96 97 98 99 / 5 4 3 2 1

Library of Congress Cataloging-in-Publication Data
Goetting, Ann.
    Homicide in families and other special populations / Ann
Goetting.
        p.   cm.
    Includes bibliographical references and index.
    ISBN 0-8261-8770-6
    1. Homicide—United States.   2. Homicide—United States—
Prevention.   I. Title.
HV6529.G64   1994
364.1'523'0973—dc20   94-36329
                                                        CIP

Printed in the United States of America

This book is dedicated to Sandra Langley

Contents

Part IV   Child Victims

Part V   Homicidal Children

Part VI   The Elderly Offender

Permissions

Selections in this volume have been reprinted, with kind permission, from the following:

Chapter 1: *Violence and Victims 6* (2), © 1991 Springer Publishing Company, Inc.

Chapter 2: *Journal of Family Violence 4* (3), © 1989 Plenum Publishing Corp.

Chapter 3: *Journal of Interpersonal Violence 3* (1) (pp. 3–20), © 1988 Sage Publications, Inc.

Chapter 4: *Journal of Comparative Family Studies XX* (3) (pp. 341–354), © Department of Sociology, University of Calgary, Alberta, Canada.

Chapter 5: *Criminal Justice and Behavior 15* (2) (pp. 179–189), © 1988 Sage Publications, Inc.

Chapter 6: *Violence and Victims 5* (4), © 1990 Springer Publishing Company, Inc.

Chapter 7: *Journal of Family Violence 3* (4), © 1988 Plenum Publishing Corp.

Chapter 8: *Criminal Justice and Behavior 16* (1) (pp. 63–80), © 1989 Sage Publications, Inc.

Chapter 9: *Violence and Victims 7* (3) © 1992 Springer Publishing Company, Inc.

Foreword

The United States has an enormous violence problem. On an average day, over 65 people die from homicide, and more than 6,000 people are physically injured from interpersonal violence. Homicide rates among young men in America, which more than doubled between 1985 and 1991, are vastly greater than those in other Western industrialized nations. Homicide is now the second leading cause of death among 15- to 34-year-olds in the U.S. and the leading cause of death for young African-American males and females. By any measure you choose, violence has a major impact on the public health of this nation.

Despite the magnitude of this problem, daily reminders in the media, and the imprisonment of an unprecedented proportion of our population, this American tragedy continues largely unabated. We need new solutions. The public health perspective that Professor Goetting describes in this book and to which her research is directly applicable represents a new vision of how Americans can work together to prevent violence. Fundamental to this vision is a paradigm shift in our society's response to violence, from one limited to reacting to violence to one that focuses on changing the social, behavioral, and environmental factors that cause violence. From a public health perspective, the development and implementation of effective policies for preventing violence must be firmly grounded in science and attentive to unique community perceptions and conditions. Scientific research provides information essential to developing viable public policies and prevention strategies and methods for testing their effectiveness. Equally critical is the full participation of communities so that we engender a sense of ownership for the problem and its solutions. Public health seeks to empower people and their communities to see violence, not as an inevitable consequence of modern life, but as a problem that can be understood and changed.

Professor Goetting's focus on homicide in the context of a public health approach is very appropriate for several reasons. First, her research is an excellent example of the first step leading to the identification of effective prevention strategies, which is to describe accurately the epidemiologic patterns, risk groups, and risk factors associated with violence. Second, as a sociologist, she brings an important and unique disciplinary perspective to homicide and its prevention. Of particular note and relevance to sociology is the need to understand better the influence of social structure on homicide and violence. While Professor Goetting and others have documented the strong relationship between poverty and homicide, much remains to be learned about the social and psychological mechanisms through which poverty operates to produce violent behavior. Sociologists have an important role to play in contributing to this understanding, and their research will be directly relevant to the formulation of public policies seeking to mitigate the impact of poverty on violence. Third, a consistent theme of this work is the understanding of primary homicide or homicide involving people in ongoing relationships. Primary homicide and violence is a particularly important aspect of this public health problem because it is responsible for a substantial proportion of homicides and nonfatal violent injuries that occur. It is also important because childhood exposure to the violence that occurs among people who know one another, particularly in families, has a profound influence on the intergenerational transfer of violence both within and outside of the family context.

Consistent with the theme of this book is the emergence of a recent initiative at the Centers for Disease Control and Prevention (CDC) focusing on the prevention of violence against women in the context of ongoing relationships. Activities developed for this program will be directed toward achieving five broad goals: (1) *Describing and tracking the problem*. CDC will develop monitoring systems that will tell us how often violence against women occurs, which women face the greatest risk, and whether the problem is improving or worsening over time at national and local levels; (2) *Demonstrating and evaluating ways to prevent violence against women*. CDC will undertake activities to determine how effective specific interventions are in preventing violence against women and how to combine specific interventions into effective programs; (3) *Conducting a national communications effort*. CDC will work to develop education, training, and public awareness activities aimed at making people recognize that violence against women is unacceptable and that we can take steps to prevent it; (4) *Supporting a nationwide network of prevention and support services*. CDC will work to establish private/public partnerships, coalitions of national organizations, and support within state and local health departments for preventing this type of violence; and (5) *Increasing our knowledge of the causes and consequences*. CDC will support prevention-oriented research that will lead to greater knowledge of modifiable factors associated with violence against women and the development of new prevention strategies. This program will build on the body of knowledge about primary homicide and violence that pioneers like Professor Goetting and many others have helped to establish.

Socrates taught that, "Without proper knowledge right action was impossible, but with proper knowledge right action is inevitable." This volume provides the proper knowledge about patterns of primary homicide and clues to the actions needed to prevent this problem. As the demand for action to prevent violence in our society increases, this book will become an increasingly valuable resource for researchers, policy-makers, public health workers, students, and, in fact, for everyone concerned with the problem of violence.

JAMES A. MERCY, PHD
Acting Director
Division of Violence Prevention
National Center for Injury Prevention and Control
Centers for Disease Control and Prevention

Introduction: Homicide as a Public Health Problem

Over the last few decades, homicide has evolved into a critical health problem in the United States. It claims a debilitating toll on human resources. Detroit recorded 130 homicides in 1953 compared with 726 in 1992. That was with a population decline; those figures represent an increase of close to 500%. New York City's homicide tally climbed from 321 in 1953 to 1665 in 1993— again a 5-fold increase, and again with a population decline. In Los Angeles County the 1953 homicide total was 82. By 1992, the population had doubled and the number of homicides had increased over 1000% to 2512 (Barry, 1993, p. 38). Nationwide in 1991, homicides accounted for the loss of at least 26,513 lives, according to National Center for Health Statistics mortality data. When these deaths are calculated in terms of potential years of life lost, homicide ranked fourth, with 870,414. Homicide was the tenth leading cause of death for Americans; for young Blacks (15–24 years old), it was the leading cause of death. The United States, in fact, has one of the highest homicide rates of any country in the world when compared with other countries that report homicide statistics to the World Health Organization. In comparing homicide rates from different countries, it must be noted that reporting methods may differ, and that domestic and international wars may affect homicide rates in some areas.

HISTORICAL BACKGROUND

It is only recently that homicide has been recognized as a health issue. Traditionally, the judicial and penal systems alone were entrusted with the responsibility of violence control. Then in 1977, the Centers for Disease Control (CDC) formed a committee of outside experts to explore morbidity and mortality in the United States in the context of prevention (Foege, 1991). That committee popularized the practice of noting not only the leading causes of death, but also the leading causes of years lost before age sixty-five. Heart disease, cancer, and stroke lead the list of causes of death, but the leading causes of years lost prematurely are unintentional injury, cancer, heart disease, homicide, and suicide. It became clear that three of the five causes of premature death—unintentional injury, homicide, and suicide—are violence-related. As a result of this finding, the CDC established a violence epidemiology branch in 1983.

With encouragement from the CDC, the Surgeon General's 1979 *Healthy People* report (U.S. Department of Health, Education and Welfare, 1979) established the control of violence as a priority national health issue. In 1978, meetings of health professionals from around the country were conducted to develop national health objectives for the 1990s. These meetings yielded specific objectives on homicide, child abuse, and suicide rates. The year 1985 was significant in the development of public health's role in addressing violence. In October, two important conferences reflected public health's growing interest in violence prevention. The New York Academy of Medicine's "Symposium on Homicide: The Public Health Perspective" was followed by Surgeon General C. Everett Koop's "Workshop on Violence and Public Health." The recommendations of the 150 experts assembled for this second workshop were reported by the Surgeon General to the Senate Committee on Children, Families, Drugs, and Alcoholism. Regional, state, and local workshops followed to create a new awareness of the possibilities for understanding and dealing with violence that is provided by multidisciplinary approaches (Koop & Lundberg, 1992). Also in 1985, two important books were published. CDC and the University of California at Los Angeles released *The Epidemiology of Homicide in the City of Los Angeles, 1970–1979* (Loya, Mercy, Allen, Vargas, Smith, Goodman, & Rosenberg, 1985), a collaborative study of the demographic and situational patterns revealed in 4950 homicide cases; and the National Academy of Sciences and the Institute of Medicine published *Injury in America—A Continuing Public Health Problem*. This latter volume claimed that injury, both intentional and unintentional, persisted as the major unaddressed public health problem of the day. Whereas injury accounted for 4.1 million years of life lost before age sixty-five each year, heart disease and cancer combined accounted for the loss of only 3.8 million such years lost. Yet we were spending $1.6 billion per year on research for the latter, and only 7% of that amount on injury research (Foege, 1991).

The following year, 1986, the Secretary's Task Force on Black and Minority Health concluded in its *Report of the Subcommittee on Homicide, Suicide, and Unintentional Injuries* that the great majority of "excess" deaths in minority populations result from interpersonal violence and suicide (The National Committee for Injury Prevention and Control, 1989, p. 195). Also in 1986, violence was included for the first time in the encyclopedic volume, *Public Health and Preventive Medicine* (Last, 1986). Thus, within a relatively short period, homicide, as one component of the comprehensive category "injury," emerged as a public health problem.

THE LIMITATIONS OF CRIMINAL JUSTICE

The public health agenda to reduce homicide was forged in the context of the clear realization that the criminal justice system alone is incapable of controlling it. Even key criminal justice representatives have openly acknowledged the system's limitations in violence control. The first major evidence of those limitations appeared in 1974, when Robert Martinson published a preliminary summary of the results of his and his colleagues' comprehensive survey of what was known about current coerced rehabilitation programs and practices at that time. The work appeared in its complete form a year later, in 1975. The report concluded that nothing worked, and that there existed no compelling evidence of how to rehabilitate offenders and reduce recidivism. The Martinson summary piece was quickly followed by an acceptance of this conclusion by the criminal justice system in the form of a Rotary Club luncheon speech delivered by Norman Carlson (1974), Director of the Federal Bureau of Prisons. There Carlson first conceded the failure of the medical model in its ability to "diagnose" crime and "treat" offenders. More recently, the U.S. Department of Justice acknowledged in *Uniform Crime Reports* that criminal justice agencies have little or no control over the factors that cause homicide (Mercy & O'Carroll, 1988, p. 286).

America's response to its debilitating homicide rate is incarceration—and more incarceration. With over one million of our citizens in prison or jail on any given day, we have the highest rate of imprisonment in the world (U.S. Has Highest Rate of Imprisonment, 1991). And rhetoric about constructing even more prisons continues. We have known for some time that coerced rehabilitation programs do not work. It is now becoming apparent that other crime control strategies of incarceration—isolation of violent offenders from potential victims in the community and deterrence of others from committing violent crimes—are also failing to achieve desired outcomes. Recent trends in crime and in criminal justice policy responses have resulted in the near-tripling of prison populations between 1975 and 1989—with no apparent decrease in levels of violent crime (Reiss & Roth, 1993, pp. 6, 295). All this suggests that factors unrelated to criminal justice policy as it is currently enforced are instrumental in producing homicide, and that at least some of these factors can be altered by governments or individuals to instead produce a more peaceful, more productive, and healthier society. In other words, after-the-fact response is not good enough. Prevention is in order.

THE PUBLIC HEALTH MODEL: PREVENTION THROUGH EPIDEMIOLOGY

The health consequences of homicide have assumed proportions of sufficient measure to qualify it as a public health emergency (Koop & Lundberg, 1992), and relief through the efforts of the criminal justice system alone is intangible. But there is additional cause for the health community to join our nation's campaign to control homicide: public health methods expand current capacities to deal with the problem. The public health model mobilizes an all-new constituency—one that is proactive rather than reactive, and one that is visible, articulate, and activist.

The public health community is strongly oriented to prevention. Indeed, preventive strategy is one of the important ways the public health community distinguishes itself from the medical community, which focuses primarily on the care of those who have already become seriously sick or injured. To help identify preventive opportunities, the public health model distinguishes among three kinds of prevention (Last, 1980). *Primary* prevention seeks to prevent the occurrence of disease or injury entirely— usually by operating on broad features of the environment that allow or encourage the disease or injury to occur; *Secondary* prevention is concerned with identifying cases or situations early in some developmental process that will lead to disease or injury if not altered—the focus here is on reducing harm; *Tertiary* prevention intervenes after an illness has been contracted or an injury inflicted, and seeks to minimize the consequences. It seeks to repair harm. Of these three forms of preventive intervention, the public health community is most strongly committed to primary prevention. It is in this domain that epidemiology, the methodological framework of the public health enterprise, most effectively can and has targeted and altered dangerous conditions and situations. It is here that imaginative and bold policy interventions have the greatest potential for making a difference.

Epidemiology is the science through which patterns of occurrence and distribution of health-related conditions in human populations are identified in order to enhance their prevention.

The epidemiologic approach can be summarized in four inter-related steps.

Step 1. *Public health surveillance* is the development and re-finement of data systems for the ongoing and system-atic collection, analysis, interpretation, and dissemi-nation of information about who is becoming ill or getting hurt and under what circumstances.

Step 2. *Risk-group identification* mandates the identification from surveillance data and other research of persons at greatest risk of disease or injury and the places, times, and other circumstances that are associated with increased risk.

Step 3. *Risk-factor identification* involves the identification, again from surveillance data and other research, of risk factors for disease or injury.

Step 4. *Program development, implementation, and evaluation* requires that trial programs based on risk-group and risk-factor identification and preventive interventions be designed, implemented, and evaluated for desired outcome (Prothrow-Stith, 1991, p. 138; Rosenberg & Mercy, 1991, pp. 17–18).

The main assumption of the public health model is that dis-ease and injury can be prevented and should not be accepted as inevitable. Furthermore, prevention can be accomplished with-out a vaccine or "magic bullet." It can be achieved through gov-ernment intervention and through alteration of public attitudes, perceptions, and associated behavior patterns. Emphasis is placed on the fact that people can be ordered and manipulated to change. The science of epidemiology is the key to a world free of excess disease and injury. It all begins with sound data iden-tifying patterns, risk groups, and risk factors. From there, care-fully orchestrated campaigns involving government intervention, media appeals, or both—designed to alter attitudes, perceptions, and behavior—must come into play. Consider recent campaigns regarding tooth decay, alcohol and tobacco use, motor vehicle safety, sexual behavior, and exercise. All represent public health efforts based on epidemiologic research. All are designed to prevent disease and injury through government intervention (i.e., fluoridation, alcohol and tobacco excise taxes, safety-belt laws, motorcycle helmet laws, AIDS testing, age criteria for alcohol and cigarette sales, drinking-while-driving laws) and personal persuasion (public health ads). All of these campaigns have worked or are working.

Rosenberg (1988, p. 152) offers a compelling example of a debilitating health problem that was significantly modified though epidemiology before discovery of its "magic bullets." Respiratory tuberculosis (TB) was rampant in England and Wales in the early nineteenth century. It was around 1945 that effective antimicrobial therapy was developed for treating TB, and also when a preventive vaccine was developed. Knowing this, most people guessed that the decrease in respiratory TB was launched by these two "magic bullets." However, examination of the data shows that a marked decline in TB rates began more than 100 years prior to the appearance of the therapy and vaccine. In fact by 1945, the greatest decline had already occurred. What brought about the decline was first the discovery that poor nutrition, poor sanitation, poor housing, and overcrowding all contributed to the spread of TB; that awareness then led to interventions addressing these causal conditions. The "magic bullets" were not necessary to initiate the train of events leading to the drastic reduction of respiratory TB. Epidemiological analysis clarified underlying patterns, opening the way to effective intervention strategy. It becomes clear that through application of epidemiology, health problems that were facts of life for people at certain times and places are now resolved. And resolutions to more recently defined health problems are on the horizon.

THE FOCUS ON PRIMARY HOMICIDE

In claiming homicide as a public health problem, the public health community asserts that it is preventable. Skeptics argue that homicide has been taking a large toll, especially among young Black males, for a long time. That indicates, they say, that its wrath is here to stay—that nothing can be done about it (Rosenberg, 1988, p. 151). But the public health camp insists that homicide, like diseases and injuries targeted before it, can be controlled through application of epidemiology.

When considering the prevention of homicide, it is important to recognize the variation that exists among its antecedent circumstances. Homicides spring from diverse sets of social dynamics. In the interest of clarifying the preventive role of public health, Janine Jason and her colleagues (Jason, Strauss, & Tyler, 1983) differentiate between two basic types of homicide. *Primary homicides* are those not occurring during the perpetration of another crime; for them, serious injury or death are the primary motivation for the assault. These are acts of passion directed usually at an acquaintance, almost always a long-term intimate acquaintance. *Secondary homicides*, on the other hand, occur when the primary intent of the perpetrator is to commit some other crime and the homicide occurs secondarily to this activity. Usually there is no ongoing personal relationship involved. Robbery homicide is an example.

It is primary homicide that has gained the attention of public health because it represents much larger numbers—between 60% and 80% (Jason, Flock, & Tyler, 1983, p. 421; Griffin & Bell, 1989, p. 2266; Jason, Strauss, & Tyler, 1983, p. 317; Rosenfeld & Decker, 1993, p. 41), and because it has been declared by national law enforcement documents to be largely a societal problem beyond the control of law enforcement (Jason, Flock, & Tyler, 1983, p. 420). Primary homicide is mostly claimed by, and suitable to, the public health enterprise because it is amenable to prevention through epidemiology. Primary homicide typically represents the conclusion of a longstanding and clearly patterned interpersonal relationship whose violent nature had become visible long before the fatal blow. Family, friends, law enforcement, and social service agencies had been alerted to the violent or potentially violent situation. It is the long-term and patterned nature of the wounded relationship and the visibility of its violence or potential violence that render it preventable. These factors combined allow room for intervention—time to identify the recurring and perhaps accelerating violence, to predict a fatal conclusion if the situation is left unaltered, and to modify behaviors accordingly. What are needed are research-based insights into these patterns of potentially fatal interpersonal violence, knowledge of risk groups and risk factors, and demonstrated successful preventive strategies.

The fact that research is now being done on family and other forms of interpersonal violence dovetails nicely with public health's recent commitment to the prevention of primary homicide. The 1975 and 1985 national family violence surveys produced by the Family Violence Research Program at the University of New Hampshire (Straus & Gelles, 1989) coupled with some excellent feminist/qualitative work (Browne, 1987; Walker, 1979, 1989; Yllo & Bograd, 1988) have yielded general patterns of intimate violence and risk information. The refinement of these data through continued research is destined to enable, first, prediction through identification of risk groups and risk factors, and then ultimately successful intervention strategy. Larry Tifft's (1993) proposed model for primary, secondary, and tertiary prevention of wife abuse is an example of the kind of informed analysis that can be constructed from epidemiological data and of which we can expect to see more in the future.

CRIMINAL JUSTICE AND PUBLIC HEALTH: A COMPLIMENTARY BUT ESTRANGED ALLIANCE

The public health agenda greatly enhances our nation's commitment and ability to reduce homicide. As it joins the criminal justice community in that ambitious effort, homicide becomes reconceptualized as a threat to not only our senses of justice and personal security, but also to our physical and emotional health and well-being. The alliance of these two enterprises further expands the criminal justice model in terms of recognized causes of homicide and, accordingly, possible lines of attack. Homicide becomes acknowledged as springing from a little-understood, complex causal system that includes, but is not limited to, the intentions of the perpetrator. Other factors influencing individual incidents and aggregate levels of homicide include the availability and use of criminogenic commodities (such as firearms, drugs, and alcohol); the intensity of criminogenic situations (such as ongoing unresolved conflicts); and a variety of cultural factors that justify and encourage violence. It follows, then, that there are important preventive opportunities beyond those relied on by the criminal justice system. While it is both just and practical to hold offenders accountable for their acts, it may be possible to prevent such behavior or reduce its seriousness, even before knowing underlying causal mechanisms (Mercy & O'Carroll, 1988, p. 292; Reiss & Roth, 1993, pp. 19, 289; Rosenberg & Mercy, 1991, p. 26), by altering its antecedent risk factors. Through identification of these risk factors, the public health community can mobilize support for antiviolence programs from constituencies not previously utilized in such a capacity (Moore, forthcoming).

This fact highlights another way in which the public health perspective broadens homicide control efforts. An important dimension of public health is its multidisciplinary nature. In its attempt to preserve, promote, and improve health, it draws on many relevant resources that remain untapped by the criminal justice system. Public health is a multidisciplinary endeavor by virtue of the fact that no single discipline can possibly address all the factors that promote health and prevent disease and injury. Biomedical sciences, engineering, law, and behavioral sciences (such as sociology, psychology, economics, and anthropology), for example, can and do make important contributions to the public health agenda (Mercy & O'Carroll, 1988, p. 289). Their research enhances prediction, and their programs enhance prevention.

It becomes clear that at present the criminal justice response to homicide is limited to tertiary or perhaps secondary prevention. To that equation, public health adds primary prevention—

a multidiscipline-informed, efficient, practical, cost-effective, and, most importantly, powerfully humane ingredient. The pain and fear associated with our nation's current inflated rates of homicide must necessarily undermine the general well-being of our citizenry, which, in turn, cannot avoid operating counter-productively in economic and other social structural domains.

A convincing case can be made for the merging of public health with criminal justice in the pursuit of homicide control. To face homicide head-on requires that we draw from both camps, but that merging process in reality shows signs of strain. In their comparative analysis of the two perspectives, Richard Rosenfeld and Scott Decker (1993) refer to tension in the relationship. They state, "the differences are, we believe, largely complementary, and the tensions are not easily resolved because they are deeply rooted in the distinct philosophical traditions and social mandates associated with the two models" (p. 12). The National Committee for Injury Prevention and Control (1989, p. 198) refers to "differences in values, vocabulary, style, and institutional missions" and to "long-standing misperceptions." It cites the following personal communication from M.H. Moore:

> "At worst," commented a criminal justice policy analyst, "public health sees criminal justice as solely concerned with locking up individuals, rather than with prevention. Criminal justice sees public health as a naive newcomer willing to subordinate all questions of civil rights or political decision-making to its notion of health as the greatest public good. Certainly, it's not always that bad, but that does give you a sense of the tensions that must be overcome if they are to collaborate effectively." (p. 12)

Rosenfeld and Decker (1993, p. 12) and Margaret Zahn (n.d.) are optimistic that time will forge a unity. But for now, there exist no coordinated efforts between criminal justice and public health, though both parties are aware of the need. In the meantime, the public health community remains committed, and continues to conduct and seek out epidemiological analyses (such as those included in this book), and to explore effective means of prevention.

OVERVIEW OF THE BOOK

Purposes

This volume assembles under one cover an introduction to violence in general and homicide specifically as public health problems, and a collection of my previously published epidemiologic studies of primary homicide in special populations. It is designed with three clear uses in mind. First, it is intended to introduce violence as a public health problem and to make accessible some examples of related epidemiologic research. The studies contained herein demonstrate the process of identifying underlying patterns of homicide that aid in understanding who is at high-risk and what risk factors come into play. The relevance of pattern, risk-group, and risk-factor identification to prevention becomes clear.

Second, the volume is intended to inform students of criminology, interpersonal violence, and homicide, of the varied nature of the homicidal experience. Homicide is the common endpoint of many divergent pathways in terms of circumstance, interpersonal dynamics, and symbolic context. These pathways may have both unique and common causes and risk factors. This collection demonstrates the diversity of homicide.

Third, and perhaps most importantly, the studies herein can be used by educators, researchers, and decision-makers who, for various reasons, seek a detailed understanding of the types of fatal encounters described and analyzed. The originally published papers, including their bibliographies, combined with the framing materials (including updated references) added here provide a near-comprehensive set of resource materials for each topic. And, in the tradition of epidemiology, the studies that constitute this collection, in combination with other relevant data in the respective subject areas, can aid in prediction and ultimately prevention efforts conducted by the public health community.

The Detroit Homicide Project

The Detroit homicide project that yielded this collection of profiles materialized and succeeded in the context of a series of fortuitous events and circumstances. It sprung from one of those once-in-a-lifetime opportunities afforded only a few social science researchers. At the 1983 annual meetings of the American Sociological Association, I served on a panel with Don Bachand, a criminologist at Saginaw Valley State University. A conversation between us led to the disclosure of his recent retirement from the Detroit (Michigan) Police Department as a homicide detective. The opportunist in me pressed for access to some of those files—just enough to produce a profile of approximately 50 elderly homicide offenders. Don connected me well, and during the summer of 1984 I was granted permission to electronically copy liberally from the files of all 1982–1983 cases in which the suspect was 55 years of age or older. With the relentless help of Gilbert Hill, then Commander of the Homicide Division, I returned during the next three summers to sift through and copy records, enabling the completion and publication in various scholarly journals of a 9-paper series on homicide among special populations. There, year after year, I sat planted at my designated table just outside the interrogation room—that is, except for when I was waiting in line at or using the fifth-floor electronic copier. During that last summer, in 1987, my presence and agenda were discovered by hostile administrative interests, and access was terminated midstream. With much to-do, I won a battle for reinstatement for the completion of just that summer's work. They thought that my annual ritual of filling my car trunk with—and transporting to Kentucky—these confidential records represented an outrageous oversight on the part of the Department. I must agree. I was just lucky. The fruits of that luck, labor, and support are reprinted here.

The plan was to produce a collection of inclusive, accurate, and sociologically detailed homicide profiles. Arrest data best represent the homicide experience when compared with court and prison data because the subjects are less filtered by criminal justice system discretion. Local arrest records yield information on more variables and with greater accuracy than do national-level arrest data supplied by the FBI through *Uniform Crime Reports* (UCR) and Supplemental Homicide Reports (SHR) (Campbell, 1992a, p.100), but the local data are, of course, far less representative. It should be noted that all information based on police records (including UCR and SHR data and the profiles contained in this volume), as well as court and prison data, are limited in terms of validity and reliability by virtue of the fact that they are, to various degrees, products of the diverse interpretations and case reconstruction abilities of the reporting officers (Cazenave & Zahn, 1992, pp. 87–88; Jurik & Gregware, 1992, p. 194). Some homicide studies have relied solely on coroner records. Those data are limited in sociological texture and are subject to the same validity and reliability problems characteristic of police records.

One important concern about using Detroit as a single site for data collection was generalizability of findings. Detroit is an urban, predominantly Black location with an inordinately high homicide rate. That fact imposes an important limitation on the research. In 1980 (the census year immediately preceding the homicides included in this study), 63% of the Detroit population was Black and, consistent with United States homicide in general, Blacks were overrepresented in the homicide drama. Of all arrestees for homicides committed in that city during 1982 and 1983, when most incidents under observation here occurred, 89.1% were Black, and 81.9% of victims were Black.

The overrepresentation of Blacks in homicide has been addressed in the research literature. Results are consistent in indicating that when socioeconomic status is taken into consideration, the disparity between Blacks and the general population as both perpetrators and victims becomes quite small. Thus, although race is associated with homicide, socioeconomic status is the more important risk factor (The National Committee for Injury Prevention and Control, 1989, p. 197). It becomes clear, then, that it is mostly because Blacks are disproportionately poor that their homicide rates are so high. Hence, it is relatively safe to conclude that the profiles contained in this volume represent "poor, inner-city" homicide to a much greater extent than they represent "Black homicide." In fact, there exists little "Black homicide" per se. Investigation into the structures and processes associated with that small portion of Black homicide that remains independent of social class is a fertile area for research. Perhaps Jacqueline Campbell's (1992a, p. 110) concept of "cultural orientation" would be a useful analytical tool.

Organization of the Book

This book contains a collection of nine profiles of homicide in special populations. Each profile relates to females (women and girls), children, or the elderly in the capacity of offender or victim, or both. The material is organized into six parts. Part I focuses on females as victims and includes a general profile, "Female Victims of Homicide: A Portrait of Their Killers and Circumstances of Their Deaths" followed by a piece more narrow in scope, "Men Who Kill Their Mates: A Profile." Part II, Homicidal Women, offers a single chapter of general coverage, "Patterns of Homicide Among Women." Part III consists of two chapters that focus on females as both victim and offender. "Patterns of Marital Homicide: A Comparison of Husbands and Wives" is followed by "When Females Kill One Another: The Exceptional Case." Next, the focus transfers from females to children. Two chapters on child victims appear in Part IV: "Child Victims of Homicide: A Portrait of Their Killers and the Circumstances of Their Deaths" followed by "When Parents Kill Their Young Children: Detroit 1982–1986." Part V, Homicidal Children, offers one chapter of general coverage, "Patterns of Homicide Among Children." Finally, the focus again transfers, this time from children to the elderly. Part VI, the Elderly Offender, includes a single chapter, "Patterns of Homicide Among the Elderly."

Each of the six parts of the book is introduced with a conceptual overview and an updated review of literature. The volume closes with a conclusion intended to illuminate preventive considerations, some applicable to violence and homicide in general, and others limited in relevence to the profiles contained herein.

CONCLUSION

The public health community has declared violence in America as a public health emergency (Koop & Lundberg, 1992) and remains committed to reducing its excesses, mostly through primary prevention. Homicide, of course, is the most extreme and visible outcome of interpersonal violence, and a priority of the public health antiviolence campaign. Of central importance to the development of effective primary prevention strategy is knowledge of and the resulting ability to predict which people are at greatest risk of involvement as both offenders and victims, and which locations, times, and other circumstances are associated with increased risk. The primary prevention of homicide, therefore, is dependent upon epidemiologic research such as the profiles outlined in this volume to enhance the accuracy of prediction. It is primary homicide—that which involves ongoing interpersonal relationships—that is targeted by public health and that is also the focus of this book.

The primary prevention of primary homicide is a lofty goal, indeed, but certainly worthy of required efforts and resources—especially in light of the fact that homicide represents only the tip of the assaultive injury pyramid. It is estimated that in 1990 only about 1 in every 257 violent victimizations was fatal to the victim. This estimate reflects an increase from about 1 in every 287 in 1988 (Reiss & Roth, 1993, p. 61). It becomes clear that in the pursuit of the primary prevention of homicide, moderate or even minor success would represent relief from the pain and expenses of more violence than meets the proverbial eye.

Female Victims

I

Introduction to Part I

The first of the two chapters in this section of the book, "Female Victims of Homicide: A Portrait of their Killers and the Circumstances of their Deaths" (Chapter 1), provides a comprehensive profile of homicides against females. It is comprehensive in the sense that it includes all female homicide victims rather than a subgroup such as those killed by a mate. In the introduction to that chapter, I state that "Nowhere in recent scholarly literature does there exist a systematic description of patterns of homicide against women." I was deploring the lamentable scarcity of such important work, and proclaiming the profile as the first of its kind. Now, five years later, there are two replications (Silverman & Kennedy, 1993, pp. 200–207 [Canada]; Smith & Brewer, 1992).

A clue to the explanation for this seeming lack of epidemiologic interest in the general female homicide victim surfaces in the work of Robert Silverman and Leslie Kennedy (1993, p. 200), where it is suggested that because the family-related portion of female victimization is high, the concept of female victimization has become synonymous with family violence. Perhaps at least partially because the majority of these domestic killings are perpetrated by mates, nearly all victimization research on females locates them in the context of mate-generated homicide. However, one-third of female homicide victimizations occur outside of the family context and nearly half are not spouse-generated

(Silverman & Kennedy, 1993, p. 205). We remain ill-informed about the violent deaths of these girls and women.

Chapter 2, "Men Who Kill Their Mates: A Profile," highlights incidents perpetrated by both current and former husbands (legal and common-law), and unmarried relational partners. Only one epidemiologic study focusing on that type of homicide was located. From an analysis of 52 selected case-comparison studies, Gerald Hotaling and David Sugarman (1986) identified clusters of risk markers associated with fatal assaults of men on their mates. Other research compares homicidal men with homicidal women. That literature is reserved for coverage in the introduction to Part III, which focuses on females as both victims and offenders and includes a comparative analysis of homicidal husbands and wives (Chapter 4).

There is clear need for replication of the comprehensive profile of homicides against females provided in Chapter 1. Empirical replication using subject pools drawn from different geographic regions would establish a clear understanding of the full spectrum of interpersonal encounters that are fatal to girls and women. The next step would be to explore in great depth, through use of diverse qualitative methods, the important subgroups identified by these comprehensive profiles. Women killed by mates represent a subgroup of great theoretical and practical significance, and that subject has gained broad research attention. But there are other subgroups worthy of consideration. Some surface in Chapter 1, while others remain unidentified. For example, as women and girls continue to be drawn into the street drug market, a pattern of their victimization in that context will emerge.

Female Victims of Homicide: A Portrait of Their Killers and the Circumstances of Their Deaths

1

There has been a renewed interest in the status of women in this country since the early 1960s, and with it has emerged considerable research attention devoted to women as victims of violence. In the context of this observation, it is of interest to note the virtual absence of scholarly effort directed toward the study of what may be considered the most serious form of interpersonal violence against women: that is, homicide. This is true even though over one in every four reported homicide victims (25.2% in 1988) is a female. What is particularly surprising is that even less is written about women as victims of homicide than about homicidal women; this is so in spite of the facts that women far more frequently are victims than perpetrators of homicide, and much more information is available to researchers on homicide victims than offenders (Wilbanks, 1981).

Nowhere in recent scholarly literature does there exist a systematic description of patterns of homicide against women. The purpose of this study is to modify this void. The analyses outlined in these pages document through use of police records the circumstances surrounding homicides against women. This chapter is designed to contribute to the development of a data base on women as victims of violence, particularly homicide, in the interest of prevention through knowledge. The findings outlined here may also prove useful to scholars and practitioners in the development of programs, treatment modalities, and services designed for the particular needs of the survivors of such fatal dramas.

The information reported herein is presented through use of a four-part organizational scheme: Demographic and Social Characteristics of Offenders and Victims, Demographic and Social Relationships Between Offenders and Victims, Circumstance of Offense, and Arrest Disposition. The chapter closes with explanatory insights and preventive considerations.

RESEARCH METHODS

This is a study of homicide against females with a focus on the offender, the victim–offender relationship, and the circumstances of offense. The subjects selected include all arrestees[1] accused of homicides against females (except for those offenses associated with the negligent use of a vehicle) committed in the city of Detroit, Michigan, during 1982 and 1983. An important limitation of the study lies in its lack of generalizability; its subjects are drawn from an urban, predominantly Black location with an inordinately high homicide rate. In fact, Detroit has long been known as the nation's murder capital (Morganthau, 1989). The study population includes a total of 131 offenders associated with the slaying of 123 victims. These 131 offenders represent 18.1% of all homicide arrestees in that city during those two years.

The data collection process took place in June of 1986 in the offices of the Homicide Section of the Detroit Police Department. Police-recorded information regarding each case, including the Investigator's Report, Interrogation Record, and Witness Statements was electronically copied for subsequent perusal. The data were tabulated and, when feasible, comparisons are made with the total population of Detroit arrestees for homicides committed during 1982 and 1983, and also through use of previous homicide studies that did not control for gender of victim and therefore based their findings on cases involving mostly male victims. Since the proportion of homicide arrestees accused of having killed females in this country remains between 17.1% and

24.9%, this means that the comparisons employed should have, according to the laws of probability, utilized populations and samples where between 75% and 83% of the members were accused of having killed males. Clearly the comparisons applied to this study are less than ideal on two counts: (a) in terms of victim gender, the comparison criterion, the groups under comparison are not totally mutually exclusive (i.e., the groups of offenders against males contain some offenders against females) and (b) except when 1982 and 1983 Detroit data are available, the groups under comparison are not comparable in terms of spatial and temporal characteristics.

ANALYSES

Demographic and Social Characteristics of Offenders and Victims

Race. Research repeatedly has verified that homicide offenders and their victims are disproportionately Black. Detroit provides no exception to this generalization, and neither do the offenders against females in the city. In 1980, 63% of the Detroit population was Black (U.S. Bureau of the Census, 1983). Of all arrestees for homicides committed in Detroit during 1982 and 1983, 89.1% were Black, and 81.9% of slain victims were Black. Information on the offenders against females in that population indicates that a lower proportion of both killers and their victims (85.5%, or 112, and 76.4%, or 94 respectively) were of that racial category. These data suggest that while offenders against females and those female victims are disproportionately Black, they are less likely to fall into that minority status than are offenders against males and their victims.

Sex of Offender. Most homicide offenders are male, and again, Detroit data are consistent with that generalization. Approximately 82% of arrestees in that city during 1982–83 were male. For the perpetrators against females, the proportion of males slightly surpassed that figure to 88.5% (116). This makes sense in light of the firmly established fact that when females kill, they almost always kill males (Goetting, 1988b, p. 181). In other words, male victims more commonly have female perpetrators than do female victims. It follows, then, that female victims will have a higher concentration of male perpetrators than will male victims or the general population of homicide victims.

Age. The study population of offenders ranged in age between 13 and 74 years, having a mean of 32.1 years of age. Their victims closely approximated that mean age (32 years), showing variation ranging from 2 months to 84.3 years. These figures do not vary considerably from those describing the general population of arrested killers and slain victims in Detroit during 1982 and 1983. There the mean arrestee and victim ages were 31.4 and 35 years of age, respectively.

Domestic and Parenthood Status of Victim. Almost half (48.5% or 40) of the 101 victims for whom information was available were married (legal or common-law) and living with their husbands at the time of the homicide. Another 13.9% (14) were children still residing with their parent(s), and 1 (1%) was a Catholic nun. The remaining 36.7% (37) were unmarried adults. Forty-six of the 51 (83.6%) victims at risk of motherhood (aged 13 and older, excluding the nun) for whom data were recorded had living child(ren) at the time of their deaths. This means that 65.7% of the total population of 70 victims for whom information was available were mothers.

Social Class Indicators of Offender. Of the 97 offenders aged 18 and older for whom information on formal education was available, 47.5% (46) had completed at least 12 years of school. Approximately 12% (12) were educated beyond that level. These data reflect a somewhat depressed level of formal education when compared with the general population of United States Blacks at the same point in time.[2] Employment information was recorded for 104 of the arrestees who were 18 years of age and older at the time of the homicide. Over two-thirds of these offenders (68.3% or 71) were unemployed, 4 reporting to be retired, and

1 claiming disability compensation. These data on education and unemployment, in conjunction with the fact that 26 of the 100 subjects for whom information was available reported having no residential telephone,[3] are congruent with other studies suggesting that homicide offenders are concentrated in the lower social classes (Bensing, Schroeder, & Jackson, 1960, pp. 128–129; Swigert & Farrell, 1978, p. 193; Wolfgang, 1958, pp. 36–39).

Arrest Record of Offender. Homicide records indicate that over four-fifths (80.2% or 81) of the 101 offenders aged 15 or older for whom data were available had been arrested in that city before the homicides that precipitated them into the study population. While this is a crude measure of criminal history, since it fails to delineate the particular charges and dispositions associated with arrests, it does suggest that a high proportion of the killers under observation here are likely to have had criminal backgrounds. This 80.2% is somewhat high when compared with general populations of homicide offenders on this dimension. Wolfgang (1958, p. 175) reports 64% and Swigert and Farrell (1978, p. 194) report 56% of their homicide offender populations as having had previous arrests.

Demographic and Social Relationships Between Offenders and Victims

Prior Social Relationship. Most reported killings in this country occur between persons having had some prior relationship. Between 1980 and 1985 only 13.3% to 17.6% of homicides involved persons unknown to one another. In Detroit during 1982 and 1983, 19.1% of the 628 homicidal relationships[4] for which information has been recorded were categorized as "strangers." The proportion associated with offenders against females is somewhat larger. Twenty-two percent (29) of the 132 relationships for which data were available were that of stranger. Another 21.2% (28) were characterized by acquaintanceship and 2.3% (3) by friendship. Approximately 21% (28) were marital relationships, including both legal and common-law, and another 15.2% (20) involved former spouses and other romantic attachments (2 of which were homosexual). In nine cases (6.8%) young girls were victimized by a parent (five by the mother), and in another four (3%), by a step-parent or parent's lover. Eight women (6.1%) were killed by their children (one by a daughter), and one each (.8%) by her sister, her niece, and her nephew. A recapitulation of these figures indicates that 54.6% (72) of the prior social relationships characterizing this population of offenders against females and their victims were domestic and/or familial in nature. This proportion is somewhat higher than the 43% and 40%, respectively, discovered by Wilbanks (1981, p. 4) and McClain (1982, p. 268). These data suggest that a higher proportion of female than male victims may be slain by strangers and by intimates, leaving fewer to be victimized by friends and acquaintances.

Residential Relationship. For over 29% (40) of the 137 homicidal relationships for which information was available, the offender and victim shared residence at the time of the offense. This proportion is high when compared with the 26.5% associated with elderly offenders (Goetting, 1992) and the 16.4% associated with child offenders (Goetting, 1989), and low when compared with the 48.6% associated with female offenders (Goetting 1988a), all in the same city during the same period. These data indicated that women are more likely to be involved with intimates as both offenders and victims in the homicide drama than are elderly and child offenders.

Demographic Relationships: Race, Sex, and Age. Homicide offenders and their victims are nearly always of the same race (Woodrum, 1990). In Detroit during 1982–83, 91.4% of the 669 homicidal relationships for which information is available were intraracial: 82.7% were Black-on-Black, and the remaining 8.7% were White-on-White. The present study indicates that a slightly lower proportion of the homicidal relationships under observation here, 87% (120), was intraracial; 71.7% (99) were Black-on-Black and the remaining 15.2% (21) were White-on-White. This slightly lower proportion is consistent with the earlier stated finding that a slightly higher proportion of these slain females than their male counterparts were killed by strangers (strangers are more likely to be of a different race than are nonstrangers).

All of the 18 cases (13%) where females were killed across racial lines were Black-on-White. This finding is consistent with information describing the general population of Detroit homicides during that time period and with findings of the other homicide studies cited above, all of which demonstrate a higher proportion of Blacks killing Whites than vice versa. The 1982–83 general homicide data show that 6.4% of those killings were Black-on-White, and 2.1% were White-on-Black. Homicide usually occurs between members of the same sex; this is because homicides typically involve males killing males. But this generalization that homicide is intrasexual does not apply to those incidents where victims are female; this is because female victims are also usually killed by males (Wilbanks, 1982, p. 152; Woodrum, 1990). In Detroit during 1982–83 only 11.6% (16) of the offenders against females were female.

Difference in age between offender and victim is another variable that may distinguish homicidal relationships involving offenders against females from those involving the general population of homicide arrestees. Approximately 38% (53) of the relationships constituting this study population of offenders against females involved a victim older than her slayer. This is a somewhat lower proportion than the 47.5% associated with the general population of arrestees for Detroit during the same time period. Perhaps this age difference can be explained by the fact that a substantial proportion of offenders against females victimizes their wives or lovers, who, by traditional standards, are the same age or younger than they.

CIRCUMSTANCES OF OFFENSE

Homicidal Motive

Most homicides arise from domestic discord and from petty quarrels between friends, neighbors, and acquaintances. Relatively few involve strangers, are committed in the act of another felony, or are rooted in other homicidal motives (Bensing, Schroeder, & Jackson, 1960, pp. 72–77; Curtis, 1974, p. 66; Swigert & Farrell, 1978, p. 199; Wolfgang, 1958, p. 191). In cases of domestic discord, the death blow is typically the culminating event in a long history of violent interpersonal tensions. The trivial issues over which people kill are often a source of amazement for the general community (Daly & Wilson, 1988, pp. 124–126).

Regarding the study at hand, 39.2% (51) of the 130 homicidal relationships for which information was available found their conclusions in the context of a domestic argument or confrontation. An additional 12.3% (16) were terminated in a nondomestic quarrelsome milieu, with 10% (13) involving friends, neighbors, or other acquaintances, and the remaining 2.3% (3) involving strangers. Another quarter (25.4%, or 33) of the homicides occurred in the context of burglary, robbery, or theft. In 7.7% (10) of the cases, death could be attributed to a psychotic reaction, and in 6.9% (9) to impatience with a young child. Another 1.5% (2), of these deadly exchanges were nondomestic and motivated by revenge, and the same proportion were attempts to prevent the victims from identifying their killers as participants in a drug-related contract murder witnessed by them. In one case (0.8%) the violence (including rape) imposed upon a 10-year-old girl appears to have been motivated by sadistic pleasure derived from the act. Finally, in one case (0.8%) a bullet found the wrong victim, and in four others (3.3%) injury was totally accidental (as determined by this researcher).

Homicidal Method

Firearms are the most common means of inflicting death in this country. Between 1968 and 1978 the proportion of homicides carried out through this method varied between 63% and 65.7% (Petrie & Garner, 1990, p. 165; Riedel, Zahn, & Mock, 1985, p. 48). In Detroit during 1982–83, 65.8% of the 1138 reported homicides were executed with firearms. Another 17.8% were stabbings, 11.4% were beatings, or 0.7% were burnings and 4.2% were conducted by some other means. For those incidents involving female victims only, a somewhat lower proportion of victims (53.7% or 66) died of gunshot wounds. A proportion very close to that of the comparison group, 18.7% (23), was stabbed. Nineteen victims (15.4%) were beaten to death, 9 (7.3%) with blunt instruments, and 10 (8.1%) through use of hands and/or feet as weapons; and another 11 (8.9%) were strangled or suffocated. One victim (.8%) was drowned, and two (infant twin daughters) (1.6%) were allowed to die of neglect. Finally, one elderly woman (.8%) suffered a heart attack resulting from emotional trauma associated with a robbery.

Number of Victims and Offenders

Almost all homicides are one-on-one incidents. Detroit provides no exception to this generalization, and neither do the offenders against females in that city. In Detroit during 1982 and 1983, 87.9% of the 578 homicides for which information is available involved a single victim and a single offender. Another 10.6% of those offenses were single-victim/multiple-offender offenses. The population of homicides against females demonstrated a lower proportion of single-victim incidents, and accordingly a higher proportion of multiple-victim incidents. Approximately 72% (89) of these killings involved a single victim and multiple offenders, including seven cases of two offenders and one case of four. Nearly 15% (18) of the deadly events were multiple-victim/single-offender in nature, 15 involving two victims, and 3 involving three victims. Finally, 8 homicides (6.5%) involved multiple victims and offenders.

Victim Precipitation

The concept of victim precipitation originated with von Hentig in the 1940s, who observed that "the victim shapes and molds the criminal" and that "the victim assumes the role of a determinant" (von Hentig, 1948, pp. 383–85, cited in Wolfgang, 1958, pp. 245–46). The actual term "victim precipitation" was later coined by Wolfgang (1958, p. 252) and is applied to those offenses in which the victim is the first in the homicide drama to use physical force directed against his/her subsequent slayer. Information on victim precipitation could be gleaned from 1982 and 1983 Detroit police records for 103 homicidal relationships involving female victims. Approximately 8% (8) of these cases were victim precipitated. This proportion is extremely low when compared with data from studies of general homicide populations, which report victim precipitation to characterize between 22% and 37.9% of deadly encounters (Curtis, 1974, p. 83; Voss & Hepburn, 1968, p. 506; Wolfgang, 1958, p. 254), but it is consistent with Wolfgang's (1958, p. 256) finding that only 6.5% of offenses against females were victim precipitated.

Spatial Considerations

A survey of homicide research suggests that between 42% and 53% of homicides occur at some private residence (Pokorney, 1965, p. 481; Riedel, Zahn, & Mock, 1985, p. 64; Swigert & Farrell, 1978, p. 199; Wolfgang, 1958, p. 123). This Detroit study suggests that offenders against women are more likely to kill in that setting than are other offenders. Over three-quarters (77.2% or 95) of the incidents under observation here took place in a home: one-third (41) occurred at the residence of the victim, 10.6% (13) at the residence of the offender, 30.9% (38) at the residence of both, and 2.4% (3) at another residence. Additionally 14.6% (18) of the incidents took place on public streets; 3.3% (4) in a bar, and 1.6% (2) in other commercial structures. Finally, 1.6% (2) occurred in churches, and 0.8% (1) at each victim's place of work and the basement of an apartment complex. This apparent difference between female and male victims is consistent with Wolfgang's (1958, p. 123) finding that female victims were over 22% more likely than were their male counterparts to be killed at a private residence.

Nearly 14% (10) of the 73 Detroit offenses committed at a private residence for which information was available occurred outside the actual residence, usually on the porch or in the yard. Approximately 40% (29) occurred in a bedroom, 15.1% (11) in the living room, 9.6% (7) in the kitchen, 6.8% (5) in a bathroom, 5.5% (4) in each the basement and a hallway, 1.4% (1) in the dining room, and 2.7% (2) in an "other" room. Again these data conform closely with those reported by Wolfgang (1958, p. 123).

Temporal Considerations

Clearly there is a temporal order inherent in violent behavior. While the tempo of homicide varies slightly according to season, it varies markedly by days of week and hours of day. Homicide is a leisure-related activity, and is closely associated with periods typically devoted to recreation.

For 1982 and 1983 combined, the frequency distribution of all Detroit homicides over the 12 months indicates a general overall stability except for slight increases during August–September (the hot season) and December–January (the holiday season), and a discernable dip in April (the introduction to spring). The female victims, however, displayed no apparent seasonal fluctuations. Their frequencies over the 12 months appear to be randomly distributed, with a high of 13.1% in September to a low of 3.3% in July.

Relative to days of week and hours of day, the research population conformed loosely to the norm. Data are consistent in indicating that homicide is concentrated during weekends (Bensing, Schroeder, & Jackson, 1960, p. 11; Voss & Hepburn, 1968, p. 504; Wolfgang, 1958, p. 107), and these offenders against women provide no exception to that generalization. But where the range of offenses occurring on Fridays, Saturdays, and Sundays reported by studies using general populations of offenders extends to between 56.6% and 84%, the proportion associated with the 112 killings for which data were recorded for this population is only 53.9% (60).

Wolfgang (1958, p. 108) and Pokorney (1965, p. 482) provide the only two sources of information that can be compared directly with data describing these Detroit killers on the subject of time of offense.[5] The two studies are consistent with one another in indicating that approximately one-half of homicides occur between 8:00 P.M. and 1:59 A.M., and another quarter occur between 2:00 P.M. and 7:59 P.M. For this population of offenders against females, significantly fewer than half (38.3% or 41) of the 107 homicides for which information was available, were executed between 8:00 P.M. and 1:59 A.M., though the expected 25.2% (27) occurred between 2:00 P.M. and 7:59 P.M. The remaining 36.4% (39) of the cases apparently were evenly distributed throughout the remaining hours of the day.

Alcohol Consumption

Available information suggests that alcohol consumption contributes to the homicide drama (Wolfgang, 1958, pp. 134, 167; MacDonald, 1961, pp. 18–20; Collins, 1981, pp. 5, 7–11, 14; Riedel, Zahn, & Mock, 1985, p. 19). The information gleaned from Witness Statements for this study of offenders against women is limited in that data were available for fewer than one-third of the subjects. But these data suggest that alcohol may have played a role in many of the incidents. At least 28.2% (37) of this research population of offenders had been drinking prior to the homicide, as had at least 29.7% (33) of their 111 victims who were age 15 or older.

Audience and Offender's Response

Over 41% (49) of the 118 victims for whom data were recorded received their fatal blows before witnesses. Most (65% or 76) of the 117 offenders for whom information was available fled the homicide scene to avoid detection. Another 6 (5.1%) committed suicide at the scene.

ARREST DISPOSITION

Prosecuting Attorney

Prosecuting attorneys are recognized as yielding weighty influence in the determination of criminal processing outcomes

(Reiss, 1974). They are allowed much discretion in their decisions as to what criminal charges, if any, will be filed against arrestees in court. Of the 121 offenders for whom information was available who were at risk of prosecution (excluding the 6 suicides and the juvenile outside the purview of the criminal justice system), 11.6% (14) were denied a warrant for criminal charges by the prosecutor. This proportion suggests a strong bias against this population of offenders in light of the fact that an estimated 30.4% of the general population of homicide arrestees for that city during 1983 enjoyed similar denial.[6] Further analyses controlling for severity of offense and other factors are necessary in order to properly question prosecutorial bias as it may apply to homicide offenders against women.

Court

Court dispositions associated with the 103 arrested adults for whom data were recorded who were processed by the court (excluding the 3 subjects never taken into custody, the 6 suicides, and the 1 subject who skipped bond) indicate that 74.7% (78) were convicted of Murder or Manslaughter; 8.7% (9) were convicted of another felony, including Assault with Intent to Do Great Bodily Harm Less than Murder and Cruelty to a Child; 2.9% (3) were convicted of a misdemeanor including Careless Discharge and Intentionally Pointing a Firearm Without Malice; and 12.6% (13) were acquitted. Of the 90 convicted arrestees 84.4% (76) received prison sentences with a mean of 12.9 years. A total of 70 of the 78 offenders convicted of Murder or Manslaughter (89.7%) were sentenced to incarceration. Six other felony convicts received prison sentences.

CONCLUSIONS

The construction of a statistical profile describing the population of all 131 persons arrested for killing females in the predominantly Black city of Detroit, Michigan, during 1982 and 1983 yields the image of a locally born Black Detroit man in his early thirties who is a Protestant, unmarried (legally or by common-law) parent living in a family setting. He is undereducated, un-employed, and has an arrest record. His relationship with a slightly younger female family member or lover, also Black and also a parent, is severed abruptly by a gunshot in a bedroom or living room of a private residence on a weekend.

It appears from this Detroit study population that while offend-ers against females are subject generally to homicidal patterns characteristic of other killers, they perhaps deviate somewhat from those norms along certain dimensions. They may less likely be Black, more likely be male, and more likely have an arrest record. They may more commonly victimize strangers and inti-mates (as opposed to friends and acquaintances). Their offenses more commonly may be interracial, and less commonly involve a victim older than the offender. A higher proportion of their of-fenses are cross-sexual. These offenders against females may be less likely to employ firearms, and more likely to beat and strangle or suffocate their victims. A lower proportion of their offenses may involve a single victim (as opposed to multiple victims), and a lower proportion may be victim precipitated. These offenders against females may more likely kill in a private residence, and may show no seasonal fluctuation in their homicidal activity.

The tragic scenarios from which these data are derived reflect life circumstances and styles that are inadequate and unaccept-able by most, if not all, standards of human existence. As one peruses these police records describing homicide offenders against females, what emerges is the portrayal of a person dis-advantaged along multiple dimensions, and in many ways iso-lated from mainstream culture. These are, for the most part, young minority fathers who are living in loosely structured fam-ily situations, and are poorly equipped to overcome their daily struggles to just get by. They are drastically limited in the educa-tional, occupational, and social resources required to maintain a life of comfort and dignity in the United States today. The women whom they victimize are of about the same social standing. For both offender and victim, knowledge of the street scene is particularly keen, though they are shrouded in ignorance regarding other areas critical to their sense of well-being. The violence described herein demonstrates what may be another cost to our society for the drastically inequitable distribution of economic resources characteristic of the United States free enterprise system.

NOTES

1. Actually, 9 subjects are not arrestees: 3 were charged by the Prosecuting Attorney for felony killings, but were never taken into custody, and 6 others committed suicide at the scene. For the purpose of this study, however, these 9 offenders are not distinguished from the arrestees.

2. In March of 1982, 54.9% of noninstitutionalized Blacks aged 25 and older in this country had completed 4 years of high school. In 1983 the comparable figure was 56.8% (U.S. Bureau of the Census, 1984–85).

3. This proportion is high when compared with the estimated 10.4% of Detroit residences reportedly having no telephone service in January of 1986 (Cross, 1986).

4. Throughout this section entitled "Demographic and Social Relationships Between Offenders and Victims," the data describing homicidal relationships characteristic of the general 1982–83 Detroit homicide population take into consideration all relationships associated not only with single-offender/single-victim killings, but also with multiple-offender and/or multiple-victim offenses. This means that the number of homicidal relationships associated with a certain analysis is greater than the number of actual homicides involved. The research population data associated with offenders against females with which these general data are compared include information on 131 offenders and 123 victims involved in 138 victim/offender relationships, including 7 double offender/single female victim, 2 triple offender/single female victim, and 2 quadruple offender/single female victim, 4 single offender/ double female victim, and 1 triple offender/double female victim incidents. Only female victims are included in the analyses. The 20 male covictims in 16 of the homicidal incidents are excluded from these

comparative analyses of demographic and social homicidal relationships.

5. Only those two studies utilized a coding scheme for hour of offense
similar to that employed for the present study.

6. The computation of this estimate can be found in an earlier Detroit
homicide study conducted by Goetting (1988a).

Men Who Kill Their Mates: A Profile

2

INTRODUCTION

While much research attention has been devoted to "wife battering" (Morash, 1986; Frieze & Browne, 1989, pp. 170–171), and some to homicidal wives acting usually in self-defense (Browne, 1986, 1989; Frieze & Browne, 1989, pp. 203–206; Goetting, 1987), virtually nothing has been written on fatal violence directed against female intimates. The purpose of this study is to modify this void. The analyses presently outlined document, through use of police records, the circumstances surrounding homicides perpetrated by men against their current and former wives and girlfriends. This chapter is designed to contribute to the development of a data base on women as victims of domestic violence, particularly homicide, in the interest of prevention through knowledge. These findings may also prove useful to scholars and practitioners in the development of programs, treatment modalities, and services designed for the particular needs of the survivors of such fatal dramas—the offenders and the families of both them and their victims.

SUBJECTS

The subjects selected for this study include the total population of 46 male arrestees accused of having killed their current

21

or former wives (both legal and common-law) or girlfriends in the city of Detroit, Michigan, during 1982 and 1983 (except for those cases attributed to the negligent use of a vehicle). (Actually, 6 subjects are not arrestees: one was charged by the Prosecuting Attorney for a felony killing, but was never taken into custody, five others committed suicide at the scene. For the purpose of this study, however, these six offenders are not distinguished from the arrestees.) Fifteen were accused of having killed legal wives, 13 of having killed common-law wives, 3 of having killed former wives (legal or common-law), and the remaining 15 of having killed current or former girlfriends. The 46 cases comprising this study population account for 6.1% of all closed homicide cases in that city during those 2 years. Data collection took place in June of 1986 in the offices of the Homicide Section of the Detroit Police Department. Police-recorded information regarding each case, including the Investigator's Report, Interrogation Record, and Witness Statements, was electronically copied for subsequent perusal.

Data on all sociologically relevant variables that could be garnered from the material were coded and tabulated. When feasible, comparisons were made with the total population of Detroit arrestees for homicides committed during 1982 and 1983, and with previous homicide studies employing general populations and samples of offenders. Since the proportion of homicide arrestees who are men accused of having killed their former or current wives or girlfriends remains between 8.2% and 9.7%, this means that the comparisons employed should have, according to the laws of probability, utilized populations and samples constituting over 90% members who are not men accused of having killed a former or current wife or girlfriend. Clearly the comparisons applied for this study are less than ideal on two counts: (1) the comparison groups are not mutually exclusive (i.e., the other-than-husband/boyfriend offender groups actually contain some homicidal husbands and boyfriends), and (2) except when 1982 and 1983 Detroit data are available, the comparison groups are not geographically and temporally comparable.

DEMOGRAPHIC AND SOCIAL CHARACTERISTICS OF OFFENDERS AND VICTIMS

Race

Research repeatedly has verified that homicide offenders and their victims in this country are disproportionately Black. Detroit provides no exception to this generalization, and neither do the men who kill their mates in that city. In 1980 (the year for which the most recent data are available), 63% of the Detroit population was Black (U.S. Bureau of the Census, 1983). Of all arrestees for homicides committed in Detroit during 1982 and 1983, 89.1% were Black, and 81.9% of victims were Black. Information on the men in that population who killed their mates indicates that 84.8% (39) of them and 82.6% (38) of their victims were of that racial category. These data suggest that homicidal men and their mates are about as likely to be Black as are other homicide offenders and their victims. One of the offenses under observation here was interracial, involving a Black man shooting his White former girlfriend.

Age

The study population ranged in age between 18 and 73 years, with a mean of 37.2 years. Their victims were in general somewhat younger, ranging from 18 to 72 years of age, with a mean of 33.7 years. These figures do not vary considerably from those describing the general population of arrested killers and slain victims in Detroit during 1982 and 1983. There the mean arrestee and victim ages were 31.5 and 35 years of age, respectively.

Religious Affiliation of Offender

Of the 20 offenders for whom data were recorded, 15 (75%) claimed a Protestant background. Two (10%) were Catholic, and the remaining three (15%) claimed no religious affiliation.

Residence and Birthplace

All except two arrestees and one of their victims were residing in the Detroit area at the time of the offense. Sixteen (53.3%) of the 30 killers for whom information was available were born in the North Central part of the United States, most (10 or 62.5% of the 16) in Detroit. Twelve (40%) offenders were Southern-born, and the remaining two (6.7%) reported having been born outside of the United States. (Using the geographic grouping of states adopted by the U.S. Bureau of the Census, the North Central region includes: Ohio, Indiana, Illinois, Michigan, Wisconsin, Minnesota, Iowa, Missouri, North Dakota, South Dakota, Nebraska, and Kansas; and the South includes: Delaware, Maryland, District of Columbia, Virginia, West Virginia, North Carolina, South Carolina, Georgia, Florida, Kentucky, Tennessee, Alabama, Mississippi, Arkansas, Louisiana, Oklahoma, and Texas.)

Family Network and Residential Mode of Offender

Nearly all of the arrestees reported having living family members. Of the 30 subjects for whom information was available, 90% (27) reported having a mother; of the 29 for whom data were recorded, 69% (20) reported having a father. Over 86% (25) of the 29 killers who supplied information on siblings reported at least 1 to be living, and 72.7% (24) of the 33 for whom data on children were available acknowledged at least 1 living child.

Most (91.7% or 33) of the 36 homicidal men who reported residential mode were living in a family setting; in fact, 47.8% (22) of the total population were residing with their victim at the time of the incident. The remaining 3 (8.3%) of the 36 offenders lived alone.

Social Class Indicators of Offender

Of the 30 offenders for whom information on formal education was available, 56.7% (17) had completed at least twelve years of school. Approximately 17% (5) were educated beyond that level, with 3.3% (1) having completed sixteen years of school. These data reflect a relatively low level of formal education when compared with the general United States population. [In March of 1982, 70.9% of the noninstitutional United States population aged 25 and older had completed 4 years of high school. In 1983, that proportion increased to 72.1% (U.S. Bureau of the Census, 1984–85).] Employment information was available for 37 of the mate-killers under observation here. Nearly 65% (24) of these men were unemployed, 3 reportedly retired.

These data on education and unemployment, in conjunction with the fact that 21.6% (8) of the 37 subjects for whom data were recorded had no residential telephone [compared with the estimated 10.4% of Detroit residences without telephone service in January of 1986; Cross (1986)] are congruent with other studies indicating that homicide offenders are concentrated in the lower social classes (Bensing et al., 1960, pp. 128–129; Swigert & Farrell, 1978, p. 193; Wolfgang, 1958, pp. 36–39).

Arrest Record of Offender

Homicide records indicate that two-thirds (22) of the 33 offenders for whom data were available had been arrested at least once prior to the offenses that precipitated them into the study population. While this is a crude measure of criminal history, since it fails to delineate the particular charges and dispositions associated with arrests, it does suggest that a high proportion of the mate-killers under observation here are likely to have had criminal backgrounds. Available research indicates a basic consistency when comparing this particular category of offender with the general population of homicide offenders on this dimension. Wolfgang (1958, p. 75) reports 64% and Swigert and Farrell (1978, p. 194) report 56% of their homicide offender populations as having had previous arrests.

CIRCUMSTANCES OF OFFENSE

Homicidal Motive

Most of the mate-killing under observation occurred in the context of domestic discord. Careful scrutiny of the police records yields a general scenario descriptive of most of the fatal incidents. Typically an argument or a physical or verbal confrontation erupts, perhaps over sexual indiscretion, money, or the threat of terminating the relationship. The death blow usually is the culminating event in a long history of interpersonal tensions entrenched in violence. It is struck in the urgency of passionate anger; the fatal outcome commonly is realized with disbelief and shock. Often the offender had not intended to go so far. These homicidal marriages and other romantic relationships appear to have been strongly ambivalent in nature, and the deadly act seems to have dissipated hateful sentiments on the part of the offender, leaving a sense of despair at the loss of a loved one.

All but 2 (95.7%) of the cases under consideration here conform to this general description. Both of the exceptions were accidental shootings. In one case, a 40-year-old White man shot his 33-year-old common-law wife in the face with a double-barrel shotgun as she entered the doorway to the basement where he and a friend were handling the weapon and discussing it in the context of an upcoming hunting trip. The offender was sentenced to 1 to 2 years in prison for Careless and Reckless Use of Firearms: Death Resulting. In the other case, a 73-year-old White man shot his 72-year-old wife to death with a handgun as their home was being burglarized by 7 young (age 15 to 22 years) Black males. For some unknown reason, the lights of the house went out during the burglary, which caused the old man to mistake his wife for a burglar. The killer was not charged with a criminal offense, but was instead employed by the state as a witness.

Homicidal Method

Firearms are the most common means of inflicting death in this country. Between 1968 and 1978, the proportion of killings committed with firearms varied between 63% and 65.7% (Riedel et al., 1985, p. 48). In Detroit during 1982 and 1983, 65.8% of the 1138 reported homicides were shootings. Another 17.8% were stabbings, 11.4% were beatings, 0.7% were burnings, and 4.2% were conducted by some other means. The distribution of homicidal methods associated with the women killed by their mates in that city during those years conforms basically to that associated with the general population of victims. Approximately 63% (29) of these women died of gunshot wounds, and 10.9% (5) were stabbed. Another 13.1% (6) were beaten to death, 10.9% (5) through use of hands and/or feet as weapons, and the remaining 2.2% (1) with a blunt instrument. Another 5 victims (10.9%) were strangled or suffocated, and 1 (2.2%) were drowned in a bathtub half-filled with water that she had prepared for herself.

Number of Victims and Offenders

Almost all homicides are one-on-one incidents, with a higher concentration among domestic killings. Detroit provides no exception to this generalization, and neither do the men who kill their mates in that city. In Detroit during 1982 and 1983, 87.9% of the 578 homicides for which information is available involved a single victim and a single offender. Another 10.6% of those offenses were single-victim/multiple-offender; 1.4% were multiple-victim/single-offender; and the remaining 0.2% were multiple-victim/multiple-offender. All except 3 (93.5%) of the homicides against mates perpetrated by men in that city during those years were one-on-one. Each of the exceptional cases involved a single offender; 2 involved 2 victims (a former girlfriend and her common-law husband; a wife and their 18-year-old daughter), and the other involved 3 (a common-law wife, her 10-year-old son, and their 8-year-old son).

Victim Precipitation

The concept and origin of the term "Victim Precipitation" was described earlier, in Chapter 1. Information on victim precipitation could be obtained from 1982 and 1983 Detroit police records for 23 homicides perpetrated by men against their mates. In only 2 of these incidents (8.7%) did the victim deliver the first blow. This proportion is extremely low when compared with data from studies of general homicide populations, which report victim precipitation to characterize between 22% and 37.9% of homicides (Curtis, 1974, p. 83; Voss & Hepburn, 1968, p. 506; Wolfgang, 1958, p. 254). However, it is consistent with Wolfgang's (1958, p. 256) finding that only 6.5% of offenses against females were victim precipitated.

Spatial Considerations

As was previously discussed, homicide research indicates that between 42% and 53% of homicides occur at a private residence (Pokorney, 1965, p. 481; Riedel et al., 1985, p. 64; Swigert & Farrell, 1978, p. 199; Wolfgang, 1958, p. 123). This Detroit study suggests, as might be expected, that men who kill their mates are more likely to kill in that setting than are other offenders. Over four-fifths (84.8% or 39) of the incidents under observation here were accomplished in a home: 28.3% (13) occurred at the residence of the victim, 10.9% (5) at the residence of the offender, 43.5% at the residence of both, and 2.2% (1) at another residence. Additionally, 15.2% (7) of the incidents took place on public streets.

Approximately 9% (3) of the 32 Detroit offenses committed at a private residence for which information was available occurred outside the actual residence (i.e., on the porch or in the yard). Nearly 47% (15) occurred in a bedroom, 12.5% (4) in each the living room and kitchen, 6.3% (2) in each a bathroom and hall-way, and 3.1% (1) in each the basement and dining room.

Temporal Considerations

Statistically, women victimized by their mates displayed an overall stability in occurence throughout the year, except for an extensive increase during August and September. Nearly 31% of the incidents occurred during those 2 months. This observation is consistent with that of Michael and Zumpe (1986), who discovered that violence by men toward women increased in the summer, and that the increases were independent of opportunity for contact between perpetrator and victim.

Relative to days of week, the study population conformed basically to the norm. Data are consistent in indicating that homicide is concentrated during weekends (Bensing et al., 1960, p. 11; Voss & Hepburn, 1968, p. 504; Wolfgang, 1958, p. 107), and these men who kill their mates provide no exception to that generalization. Just over 61% (27) of the 44 killings for which data were recorded occurred on Fridays, Saturdays, and Sundays (the days of the three highest single frequencies), which clearly is in line with the range extending between 56.6% and 84% reported by investigations using general populations of offenders. This research population deviates from the other studies, however, in that the point of highest frequency was Sunday as opposed to Saturday.

Wolfgang (1958, p. 108) and Pokorney (1965, p. 482) are the only homicide researchers who utilized a coding scheme for hour of offense similar to that employed for the present study. Their findings are consistent with one another in indicating that approximately one-half of homicides occur between 8:00 P.M. and 1:59 A.M., and another quarter occur between 2:00 P.M. and 7:59 P.M. For this population of mate-slayers, frequencies over time of day were more evenly distributed. Somewhat less than the expected half (43.2% or 19) of the 44 homicides for which information was available were executed between 8:00 P.M. and 1:59 A.M., the remaining cases were almost evenly distributed throughout the remaining hours of the day.

Alcohol Consumption

Available information suggests that alcohol consumption makes a critical contribution to marital violence (Leonard & Jacob, 1988) and to homicide (Wolfgang, 1958, pp. 134–167; MacDonald, 1961, pp. 18–20; Riedel et al., 1985, p. 19). The information gleaned from witness statements for this study population is limited in that data were available for just over a third of the subjects. But the data suggest that alcohol may have played a vital role in many of these incidents where men killed mates. At least 34.8% (16) of this total population of killers had been drinking prior to the homicide, as had at least 23.9% (11) of their victims.

Audience and Offender's Response

Over 44% (20) of the 45 offenders for whom data were recorded administered their fatal blows before witnesses. Most (65.9% or 29) of the 44 killers for whom information was available fled the homicide scene to avoid detection. Another 5 (11.4%) committed suicide at the scene.

ARREST DISPOSITION

Prosecuting Attorney

Of the 41 offenders who were at risk of prosecution (excluding the 5 suicides), 14.6% (6) were denied warrant for criminal charge by the Prosecutor. This proportion suggests a strong bias against this population of offenders in light of the fact that an estimated 30.4% of the general population of homicide arrestees for that city during 1983 enjoyed similar denial. [This estimate was computed by dividing the number of warrants issued by the Office of Wayne County Prosecuting Attorney in 1983 for Murder and Manslaughter in the city of Detroit (296) (Smith, 1985) by the total number of 1983 arrests for Murder and Manslaughter recorded by the Homicide Section of the Detroit Department of Police (425); by then transforming that quotient (.696) to a percentage by multiplying by 100 (69.6%—this represents the proportion of arrestees who were issued warrants); and by subtracting that percentage from 100 (30.4%). The estimate is vulnerable to error to the extent that some arrestees may have died before the preliminary hearing or may have been issued a warrant for a crime other than murder or manslaughter. Those cases would be incorrectly counted as having been denied a warrant, artificially inflating the true proportion of dismissals.] Further analyses controlling for severity of offense and other factors are necessary in order to properly question prosecutorial bias as it may apply to men who kill their mates.

Court

Court dispositions associated with the 39 arrestees who were processed by the Court (excluding the subject never taken into custody, the 5 suicides and 1 subject who skipped bond) indicate that 64.1% (25) were convicted of Murder or Manslaughter: 5.1% (2) were convicted of another felony including Assault with Intent to Do Great Bodily Harm Less than Murder and Careless and Reckless Use of a Firearm: Death Resulting; 2.6% (1) were convicted of a misdemeanor including Careless Discharge and Intentionally Pointing a Firearm Without Malice; and 12.8% (5) were acquitted. Of the 28 convicted arrestees, 85.7% (24) received prison sentences: 4 for life, and the rest for a mean minimum of 9.8 years. A total of 22 of the 25 convicted of Murder or Manslaughter (88%) were sentenced to incarceration. Both of the other felony convicts received prison sentences.

DISCUSSION

The construction of a statistical profile describing the population of 46 men arrested for killing their mates in the predominantly Black city of Detroit, Michigan, during 1982 and 1983 yields the image of a North Central- or Southern-born Protestant Black man in his middle or late 30s who lives in a family setting. He is an undereducated, unemployed father with an arrest record, whose final in a series of heated arguments or confrontations with his slightly younger current or former wife or girlfriend culminated in an offensive gunshot in a bedroom of one or both of their homes on a weekend.

It appears from this Detroit study population that men who kill their mates generally are subject to patterns characteristic of other homicides. The offenders under observation here deviate from established norms along very few dimensions, most notably that of victim precipitation. Comparatively few victims in this study delivered the first show of physical force against their subsequent slayers. This is consistent with what we know about women as homicide victims, however, and in that sense reflects normative behavior. This research suggests that men who kill their mates are more likely to do so at a private residence than are other homicide offenders. This finding too would be expected by virtue of the fact that these are killings involving domestic relationships. Finally, this study indicates that offenses perpetrated by men against their mates may fail to conform to the leisure-related temporal order of homicide in general. Perhaps this particular form of killing is instead subject to more subtle dynamics inherent in the mate relationship.

Insights obtained from scrutinizing the hundreds of descriptive accounts, especially witness statements, required to construct this profile transcend its abstract and depersonalized form. What emerges as one examines the documents is a portrayal of a couple who have come to incorporate violence into their regular mode of interaction. And typically, it is the woman who has been the recipient of such abuse. Clearly, there is a critical need for effective intervention and support agencies to accommodate the needs of women victimized by domestic violence. Assistance must be provided to prevent the kinds of final and fatal incidents depicted in this investigation. Research suggests that nonlethal violence precedes domestic homicide, and that a previous violent event almost always had been reported to the police (Straus, 1986, p. 457; Frieze & Browne, 1989, p. 205). Thus, homicide does not occur without warning. Police should be specifically trained in domestic concerns to heed such warning, and urged to view reported cases of domestic conflict in a more serious light (Pagelow, 1984, pp. 319–320). Also, they need to respond more effectively (Elliott, 1989, p. 428).

Available evidence suggests that continued domestic violence against women may be reduced by police arrests (Sherman & Berk, 1984) although some research raises doubts about the magnitude of the effect (Elliott, 1989). Langan and Innes's (1986) analysis of National Crime Survey (NCS) data indicates that simply reporting such violence may decrease the likelihood and severity of subsequent assaults. Only an estimated 14.4% of severe incidents of domestic violence against women are brought to police attention (Kantor & Straus, 1987). The most common reason offered by female respondents for not reporting domestic violence is that the woman considered the incident a private or personal matter (Langan & Innes, 1986; Weis, 1989, p. 129). These women need to be dissuaded from that perspective, and encouraged to seek formal intervention.

Homicidal Women II

Introduction to Part II

Chapter 3, "Patterns of Homicide Among Women," provides a comprehensive profile of homicidal women. Quite a few such profiles have surfaced over the last decade or two, yielding insights into a wide spectrum of fatal incidents perpetrated by women. It is interesting to observe that scholars focus more attention on women who kill than on women who are killed, even though far fewer women perpetrate than are victims of homicide. William Wilbanks (1982, p. 1) explains:

> Perhaps the fact that women are killed seems more "natural" than the fact that women do occasionally kill. Only the latter appears to call for an explanation. It may be that the female killer is viewed as somewhat abnormal (not feminine?) since aggression and killing is generally thought of as a male prerogative.

Ira Silverman, Manuel Vega, and Terry Danner (1993) have produced a thorough and wonderfully accessible summary profile from their careful scrutiny of 21 comprehensive studies of homicidal women. Subsequently, 5 other studies (including Chapter 3) have contributed to that research pool (Block, 1990; Jurik & Winn, 1990; Mann, 1990; Silverman & Kennedy, 1988 [Canada]).

Recent findings have offered some timely new insights into our understanding of homicidal women, suggesting productive lines of future inquiry. Kathleen Block (1990) discovered age of offender to be related to patterns of homicide somewhat independent of gender. In other words, patterns of homicide vary with offender's age somewhat differently for women than for men. Continued research on the association of age with commission of offenses could enhance our understanding of homicide for both women and men as they progress through the life cycle. Henry Brownstein and associates (1993, 1994) and Sandra Langley and associates (1993) alert us with New York prison data secured for their "Female Drug Relationships in Murder" project, that homicidal patterns of women may be changing to include a category of women who kill in the drug-market context. They suggest from their observations of such women that patriarchy as well as women's place in our nation's political economy may be important factors in the expansion of women's involvement in drug-market homicide (Brownstein, Spunt, Crimmins, & Langley, 1993, p. 20). Using police and court data, Coramae Mann (1991) provides a comparative analysis of incidents where women kill intimates, and incidents where they instead victimize acquaintances and strangers. The reported differences enlighten us to the need to better understand and identify the subtly nuanced texture of pathologically vulnerable intimate relationships as they progress to a homicidal climax.

Patterns of Homicide Among Women

3

With the last three decades' burgeoning interest in the study of women, considerable research attention has been devoted to women as victims of violence. In comparison, very little is written of violent women. This discrepancy might be explained partially by gender stereotyping: Traditional female role expectations accommodate the woman as a victim, but not as a perpetrator of violence. Another possible explanation for the limited attention devoted to female violence, however, is that women perpetrate only a very small proportion of our society's violence: Fewer than 15% of arrestees for homicide in the United States are females.

Much of the information available on homicidal women consists of psychological and psychiatric interpretations that seem to be designed to sensationalize rather than to inform. Relatively few studies, when compared with those of men, reflect concern for patterns and trends of homicide. This deemphasis of the sociological perspective applied to homicidal women is perhaps also gender based. Whereas males may be viewed as resorting to crime for economic reasons or through inadequate socialization, such behavior on the part of females may be attributed to their alleged sickness, weakness, frailty, and vulnerability (Wilbanks, 1982, p. 152). On at least two counts then, gender stereotyping may have affected researchers' approach to the subject of women and homicide.

An important methodological weakness associated with most sociological studies probing women who kill lies in the method of sample or population selection. The majority of these studies utilize incarcerated subjects (Mann, 1987, p. 160), imposing systematic bias by excluding those arrestees who were not prosecuted (or who had charges dismissed), convicted, and incarcerated, and also those suspects who were charged but never arrested. In the current study, the proportion excluded from prison exceeds 70%.

The purpose of this study, correcting for these research biases, is to provide data on violent (in particular, homicidal) women, in hopes of developing a firmer basis for prevention and intervention programs.

The current study, an analysis of police records of homicides by women, is broken into four parts: Demographic and Social Characteristics of Offenders and Victims, Demographic and Social Relationships Between Offenders and Victims, Circumstances of Offense, and Arrest Disposition. The chapter closes with some less formal observations regarding the cases under consideration.

RESEARCH METHODS

The subjects selected for this study include all female arrestees[1] for homicides (except those attributed to the negligent use of a vehicle) committed in the city of Detroit, Michigan, during 1982 and 1983. An important limitation of the study lies in its lack of generalizability: its subjects are drawn from an urban, predominantly Black population with an inordinately high homicide rate. In fact, in 1987, its third consecutive year for ranking highest in the nation, Detroit reported 54.6 homicides per 100,000 inhabitants. The study population includes a total of 136 offenders associated with the slaying of 136 victims. These 136 offenders represent 18.1% of all homicide arrestees in that city during those two years. Data collection took place in June of 1986 in the offices of the Homicide Section of the Detroit Police Department. Police-recorded information regarding each case, including the Investigator's Report, Interrogation Record, and Witness Statements was electronically copied for subsequent perusal.

Data on all sociologically relevant variables that could be gleaned from the material were coded and tabulated. When feasible, comparisons are made with the total population of Detroit arrestees for homicides committed during 1982 and 1983, and with previous homicide studies that did not control for gender and therefore based their findings on cases involving mostly male offenders. Since women account for 13% to 14% of homicide arrestees, the comparison studies used populations and samples that were 86% to 87% male. Clearly, the comparisons applied for this study are less than ideal on two counts: (1) the comparison groups are not mutually exclusive for offender gender, and (2) except when 1982 and 1983 Detroit data are available, the comparison groups are not geographically and temporally comparable.

ANALYSES

Demographic and Social Characteristics of Offenders and Victims

Race. Research repeatedly has verified that homicide offenders and their victims are disproportionately Black. Detroit provides no exception to this generalization, and neither do the homicidal women in that city. In 1980 (the year for which the most recent data are available), 63% of the Detroit population was Black (U.S. Bureau of the Census, 1983). Of all arrestees for homicides committed in Detroit during the years 1982 and 1983, 89.1% were Black, and 81.9% of victims were Black. Data revealed that 93.4% of female arrestees for homicide, *and their victims*, were Black, suggesting that homicidal women are more likely to be Black than are their male counterparts, and are more likely to select Blacks as their victims.

Sex of Victim. Most victims of homicide are male, and, again, Detroit data are consistent with that generalization. Over three-quarters (77.2%) of the 1982–1983 population of slain victims in that city were male. The proportion of male victims of females was higher: 88.2% (120).

Age. The study population ranged in age between 16 and 82 years, with a mean of 32.3 years. Their victims were in general somewhat older, ranging from 13 months to 80 years of age, with a mean age of 36.2 years. These figures do not vary considerably from those describing the sex-general population of arrested killers and slain victims in Detroit during 1982 and 1983. There the mean arrestees and victim ages were 31.5 and 35 years of age, respectively.

Religious Affiliation of Offender. Of the 76 offenders for whom data were recorded, 61 (80.3%) claimed a Protestant background. In total, 7 (9.2%) were Catholic, none was Jewish, 3 (3.9%) declared allegiance to an "other" religion, and the remaining 5 (6.6%) claimed no religious affiliation.

Residence and Birthplace. All arrestees and their victims were residing in the Detroit area at the time of the offense. In total, 76 (69.8%) of the 109 killers for whom information was available were born in the North Central part of the United States, most (61 or 80.3% of the 76) in Detroit. Of the offenders, 29 (26.6%) were southern-born, and the remaining 4 (3.7%) were born in the Northeast region of the United States.[2]

Family Network, Domestic Status, and Residential Mode of Offender. Nearly all of the arrestees reported having living family members. Of the 109 subjects for whom information was available, 74.3% (81) reported having a mother, and of the 102 for whom data were recorded, 61.8% (63) reported having a father. Nearly 93% (103) of the 111 killers who supplied information on siblings reported at least 1 to be living, and 85.1% (103) of the 121 for whom data on children were available acknowledged at least 1 living child.

Most (88.5% or 108) of the 122 homicidal women who reported residential mode were living in a family setting; in fact, over half (52.7% or 69) of those 131 reporting domestic status resided with their legal or common-law husband. Approximately 4% (5) of the 122 subjects shared residence with nonfamily. Only 7.4% (9) lived alone.

Social Class Indicators of Offender. Of the 107 offenders for whom information on formal education was available, 45.8% (49) had completed at least 12 years of school. Approximately 17% (18) were educated beyond that level, with 1.9% (2) having completed 16 years. These data reflect a relatively low level of formal education when compared with the general population of United States women and also, but to a lesser extent, with the general population of United States Blacks at the same point in time.[3] Employment information was available for 121 of the female arrestees who were 17 years of age and older at the time of the homicide. Over three-quarters of these women (76.9% or 93) were unemployed, 4 reportedly retired.

These data on education and unemployment in conjunction with the facts that 73.1% (49) of the 67 subjects for whom information was available were welfare recipients, and 27.2% (34) of the 125 for whom data were recorded reported having no residential telephone,[4] are congruent with other studies suggesting that homicide offenders are concentrated in the lower social classes (Bensing, Schroeder, & Jackson, 1960, pp. 128–129; Swigert & Farrell, 1978, p. 193; Wolfgang, 1958, pp. 36–39).

Arrest Record of Offender. Homicide records indicate that nearly two-thirds (64.7% or 55) of the 85 female offenders for whom data were available had been arrested at least once prior to the offenses that precipitated them into the study population. While this is a crude measure of criminal history, since it fails to delineate the particular charges and dispositions associated with arrests, it does suggest that a high proportion of the homicidal women under observation here are likely to have had criminal backgrounds. Available research indicates a basic consistency when comparing these women with sex-general populations of homicide offenders on this dimension. Wolfgang (1958, p. 175) reports 64% and Swigert and Farrell (1978, p. 194) report 56% of their homicide offender populations as having had previous arrests.

Demographic and Social Relationships Between Offenders and Victims

Prior Social Relationship. Most reported killings in this country occur between persons who have had some prior relationship. Between 1980 and 1985 only 13.3% to 17.6% of homicides involved persons unknown to one another. In Detroit during the years 1982 and 1983, 19.1% of the 628 homicidal relationships[5] for which information has been recorded were categorized as "strangers." Among Detroit females the proportion is significantly smaller: Only 6.7% (9) of the 134 relationships for which data were available were that of stranger. Approximately 42% (56) involved spouses, both legal and common-law, and 17.2% (23) involved former spouses and other romantic attachments (2 of which were homosexual). Another 18.7% (25) were acquaintances, 3% (4) friends, and an additional 2 (1.5%) involved unrelated housemates, roommates, or boarders. In addition, 11 small children were killed by this population of women. In 8 cases (6%) the woman victimized her own child; in 2 (1.5%), the woman killed the child of a spouse or boyfriend; and in another (0.7%), her victim was her infant foster child. The remaining 4 homicidal incidents (0.7% each) involved women killing their mother, sister, aunt, and nephew. A recapitulation of these figures indicates that over 70% (94) of the prior social relationships characterizing this female offender population and their victims were domestic and/or familial in nature. This observation is consistent with results of other research on homicidal patterns of women (Mann, 1987, Table 3; Wilbanks, 1983a, p. 304).

Residential Relationship. For nearly half (48.6% or 67) of the homicidal relationships under observation here, the offender and victim shared residence at the time of the offense. This proportion is significantly higher than those associated with two other populations of Detroit killers; during the same time span, 26.5% of elderly arrestees (Goetting, 1992), and between 1977 and 1984, 16.4% of child arrestees (Goetting, 1989) lived with their victims. This high proportion associated with women is a clear indicator of their greater tendency to victimize intimates.

Demographic Relationships: Race, Sex, and Age. Homicide offenders and their victims are nearly always of the same race (Bensing et al., 1960, p. 51; Block, 1976, p. 498; Swigert & Farrell, 1978, p. 197; Voss & Hepburn, 1968, p. 59). In Detroit during 1982 and 1983, 91.4% of the 669 homicidal relationships for which information is available were intraracial: 82.7% were Black-on-Black, and the remaining 8.7% were White-on-White. A slightly higher proportion of the homicidal relationships under observation here (95% or 131) were intraracial: 89.9% (124) of those cases were Black-on-Black, and the remaining 5.1% (7) were White-on-White. This slightly elevated proportion of intraracial killings may represent still another reflection of the woman's greater tendency to victimize family members and lovers. Of the 7 cases (5%) where women killed across racial lines, 4 (2.9%) were White-on-Black, and the remaining 3 (2.2%) were Black-on-White. These findings are incongruent with information describing the general population of Detroit homicides during that time period and with findings of the other homicide studies cited above, all of which demonstrate a higher proportion of Blacks killing Whites than vice versa. The 1982–1983 age-general homicide data show that 6.4% of those deadly incidents were Black-on-White, and 2.1% were White-on-Black.

Homicide usually occurs between members of the same sex, but this generalization does not apply to women, who almost always select men as their victims (Bensing et al., 1960, pp. 57, 64; Block, 1976, p. 498; Gibbons, 1973, p. 361; Swigert & Farrell, 1978, p. 197; Voss & Hepburn, 1968, p. 503; Wilbanks, 1983a, p. 10; 1983b, p. 304). In Detroit during 1982 and 1983, 66.4% of the 669 reported homicidal relationships were intrasexual. Whereas 80.3% of these relationships with a male perpetrator had a male victim, only 11.6% (16) of such relationships with a female perpetrator had a female victim. Consistent with other research, these data indicate that both males and females prefer to kill males.

Age is another variable that may distinguish homicidal relationships involving female perpetrators from those involving the general population of homicide arrestees. Nearly 62% (85) of those relationships associated with this study population of women involved a victim older than the slayer. This is a somewhat higher proportion than the 47.5% associated with the comparable sex-general population. Perhaps this age difference can be explained by the fact that a substantial proportion of female offenders victimize their husbands or lovers, who, by traditional standards, are older than they.

Circumstances of Offense

Homicidal Motive. Most fatal encounters arise from domestic discord and petty quarrels between friends, neighbors, and acquaintances. Relatively few are felony homicides, resultant of altercations between strangers, or rooted in other homicidal motives (Bensing et al., 1960; pp. 72–77; Curtis, 1974, p. 66; Swigert & Farrell, 1978, p. 199; Wolfgang, 1958, p. 191). In cases of domestic discord, the death blow is typically the culminating event in a long history of violent interpersonal tensions. The cheap issues for which people trade their lives in petty quarrels are often a source of amazement for the general community.

In the current study, over one-half (54.9% or 73) of the 133 homicidal relationships for which information was available found their conclusions in the context of a domestic argument or confrontation. An additional 15.8% (21) were terminated in a quarrelsome milieu, with 14.3% (19) involving friends, neighbors, or other acquaintances, and the remaining 1.5% (2) involving strangers. In 9.8% (13) of these cases, death could be attributed to defense of self or others. Another 5.3% (7) of the deadly exchanges occurred in the context of a burglary, robbery, or theft, and 4.5% (6) were the result of impatience with a small child.

This leaves 5 cases (3.8%) motivated by revenge, 3 (2.3%) by psychotic reaction, and 2 (1.5%) by insurance benefits. Finally, in 2 cases (1.5%) the victim was unintended, and in 1 case injury was totally accidental (as determined by this researcher).

Homicidal Method. As discussed earlier, firearms are the most common means of inflicting death in this country. Between 1968 and 1978 the proportion of killings committed with firearms varied between 63% and 65.7% (Riedel, Zahn, & Mock, 1985, p. 48). In Detroit during 1982 and 1983, 65.8% of the 1,138 reported homicides were shootings. Another 17.8% were stabbings, 11.4% were beatings, 0.7% were burnings, and 4.2% were conducted by some other means. The distribution of homicidal methods associated with the female component of Detroit killers during those years differs from that associated with the sex-general population primarily in that a lower proportion (52.2% or 71) employed firearms and a higher proportion (36.8% or 50) used blades. Wolfgang (1958, p. 87) discovered the same phenomenon, attributing it to "cultural tradition": Their domestic role involving food preparation makes women more comfortable with knives than with guns when compared with men, who are comfortable with both. Additionally, 10 victims of these women (7.4%) were beaten to death, 9 (6.6%) with blunt instruments, and 1 (0.7%) through use of hands as weapons against a child. In total, 1 victim was strangled, 1 suffocated, and 2 (infant twin daughters) allowed to die of neglect. Finally, 1 elderly man suffered a heart attack resulting from emotional trauma associated with a robbery.

Number of Victims and Offenders. Almost all homicides are one-on-one incidents. Detroit provides no exception to this generalization, and neither do the female killers in that city. In Detroit during 1982 and 1983, 87.9% of the 578 homicides for which information is available were one-on-one. Another 10.6% of those offenses were single-victim/multiple-offender, 1.4% were multiple-victim/single-offender, and the remaining .2% multiple-victim/multiple-offender. The population of homicides perpetrated by women did not differ significantly from the sex-general popula-

tion on this dimension. Approximately 85% (116) of these killings were one-on-one. Another 16 cases (11.8%) involved a single
victim and multiple offenders, including 9 cases of 2 offenders,
5 cases of 3, and 2 cases of 4. Finally, 4 homicides (2.9%) involved
2 victims and 1 offender.

Victim Precipitation. Information on victim precipitation
was gleaned from 1982 and 1983 Detroit police records for 117
homicidal relationships involving female perpetrators. Approximately 56% (65) of these cases were victim precipitated. This
proportion is high when compared with data from studies of
sex-general homicide populations, which report victim precipitation to characterize between 22% and 37.9% of deadly encounters (Curtis, 1974, p. 83; Voss & Hepburn, 1968, p. 506; Wolfgang, 1958, p. 254), but it is consistent with Wolfgang's (1958,
p. 255) finding that females were twice as frequently offenders
in victim-precipitated slaying as they were in non-victim-
precipitated killings.

Spatial Considerations. This Detroit study suggests that
women are more likely to kill in a private residence setting than
are men. Over four-fifths (109) of the 136 killings for which data
were available were accomplished in a home: 22.8% (31) occurred at the residence of the offender, 7.4% (10) at the residence of the victim, 47.1% (63) at the residence of both, and
2.9% (4) at another residence. Additionally 14% (19) of the incidents took place on public streets, 2.9% (4) in a bar, and another 2.9% (4) in other commercial structures. This apparent
difference between women and men is consistent with data
reported by Wolfgang (1958, p. 124) and later by Swigert and
Farrell (1978, p. 199), indicating that a higher proportion of
women offenders kill at home.

Nearly one-fifth (19.4% or 19) of the 93 Detroit offenses committed at a private residence for which information was available occurred outside the actual residence, usually on the porch
or in the yard. Approximately 28% (27) occurred in the living
room, 23.5% (23) in a bedroom, 11.2% (11) in the kitchen, 8.2%

(8) in the dining room, 3.1% (3) in each the basement and a hall-way, and 2% (2) in each a bathroom and in an "other" room.

Temporal Considerations. The women under observation here, while demonstrating somewhat less stability over time, showed an increase during December and January, and a spring lull (though in March rather than April). Unlike the sex-general population of homicides, however, those perpetrated by women showed no summer irregularity, but did show an appreciable dip in November.

Relative to days of week and hours of day, the female research population conformed closely to the norm. Data are consistent in indicating that homicide is concentrated during weekends, peaking on Saturdays (Bensing et al., 1960, p. 11; Voss & Hepburn, 1968, p. 504; Wolfgang, 1958, p. 107), and these women provide no exception to that generalization. Just over 56% (75) of the 133 killings for which data were recorded occurred on Fridays, Saturdays, and Sundays (the days of the three highest single frequencies), which clearly is in line with the range extend-ing between 56.6% and 84% reported by studies using general populations of offenders.

Wolfgang (1958, p. 108) and Pokorney (1965, p. 482) provide the only two sources of information that can be compared di-rectly with data describing these Detroit women on the subject of time of offense.[6] The two studies are consistent with one another in indicating that approximately half of deadly encoun-ters occur between 8:00 P.M. and 1:59 A.M., and another quarter occur between 2:00 P.M. and 7:59 P.M. Congruous with these sex-general homicide populations, the women under observation here executed 46.5% (60) of the 129 homicides for which information was available between 8:00 P.M. and 1:59 A.M., and 25.6% (33) between 2:00 P.M. and 7:59 P.M. The remaining 27.9% (36) of the cases apparently were evenly distributed throughout the remain-ing hours of the day.

Alcohol Consumption. Available information suggests that alcohol consumption makes a critical contribution to the homicide drama. Wolfgang (1958, pp. 134–167) observes that alcohol was present in 64% of homicide occurrences, and that both parties to the act had been drinking in 44% of the cases. MacDonald (1961, pp. 18–20) summarizes a series of studies showing that a third or more of homicide offenders were under the influence of alcohol at the time of the killing. More recently, Riedel and associates (1985, p. 19) report that for the 8 American cities under consideration, the proportion of victims testing positive for alcohol varied significantly between 38.4% and 62%. The information gleaned from witness statements for this study of homicidal women is limited in that data were available for fewer than half of the subjects. But these data reveal that alcohol remains a vital component of the homicide drama when women are perpetrators. At least 35.3% (48) of this total population of female killers had been drinking prior to the deadly incident, as had at least 47.7% (61) of their 128 victims who were age 15 or older.

Audience and Offender's Response. Nearly 45% (57) of the 127 victims for whom data were recorded received their fatal blows before witnesses. More than 69% (91) of the women under scrutiny here remained with their victims until investigators arrived. None committed, and only 1 is reported to have attempted, suicide in connection with the offense.

Arrest Disposition

Prosecuting Attorney. One factor that may affect the prosecutor's decision to convict is a tendency toward differential treatment based on gender, whereby women receive preferential treatment. While the only recent test of the "chivalry" hypothesis applied specifically to homicide data suggests that gender is not a significant predictor of prosecutorial disposition (Wilbanks, 1983b, pp. 12–13), most studies of felony defendants have found that women are more likely to be released prior to trial than their male counterparts (Gruhl, Welch, & Spohn, 1984, p. 456).

Of the 129 offenders for whom information was available, 36.4% (47) were denied warrant by the prosecutor. Since an estimated 30.4% of the general population of 1983 Detroit homicide arrestees were similarly denied warrant,[7] the chivalry hypothesis may be relevant. But the relatively high proportion of victim precipitation among these women may also help explain this small difference. Further analyses controlling for severity of offense and other factors are necessary in order to properly question prosecutorial bias as it may apply to female homicide offenders.

Court. Court dispositions associated with the 83 women for whom data were recorded who were processed by the court indicate that 81.8% (48) were convicted of Murder or Manslaughter; 2.4% (2) were convicted of another felony, including Assault With Intent to do Great Bodily Harm Less Than Murder, and Cruelty to a Child; 7.2% (6) were convicted of a misdemeanor, including Careless Discharge and Intentionally Pointing a Firearm Without Malice; and 32.5% (27) were acquitted. Of the 56 convicted arrestees, 67.9% (38) received prison sentences—1 for life, and the rest for a mean minimum of 8.2 years. A total of 36 of the 48 women convicted of murder or manslaughter (75%) were sentenced to incarceration. In total 1 felony convict plus 1 woman convicted of a misdemeanor received a prison sentence (the latter for 15 days).

CONCLUSIONS

The construction of a statistical profile describing the population of all 136 women arrested for homicide in the predominantly Black city of Detroit, Michigan, during 1982 and 1983 yields the image of a locally born, Black Detroit resident in her early 30s who is Protestant, married (legally or by common-law), and living with her family. She is an undereducated, unemployed welfare recipient with an arrest record, whose final in a series of arguments or fights with her slightly older current or former husband or lover culminated in a defensive gunshot in a private residence on a weekend between 2:00 P.M. and 1:59 A.M.

Scrutiny of the hundreds of descriptive accounts, especially witness statements, reveals the killer as a person disadvantaged along multiple dimensions, and in many ways isolated from mainstream culture. Some of these women apparently are bitter, mean, and/or exploitative, but most of them are not. They are minority mothers who, for the most part, are living in loosely structured relationships with men, and are poorly equipped to overcome their daily mundane struggles to just get by. They are drastically limited in the educational and occupational resources and in the social skills required to maintain a life of comfort and dignity in the United States today. Almost all of these women are obese and in other ways unhealthy and unattractive by media standards. Though their knowledge of the street scene is particularly keen, they are shrouded in ignorance in other areas critical to their sense of well-being. One example of such ignorance was a precipitating factor in two of the deadly incidents included in this study. Two women (in unrelated cases) who beat infants to death argued convincingly that the child had *refused* to mind by continuing to dirty his pants in spite of constant reprimands. Such behavior on the part of the child was attributed to willfulness rather than to immature psychomuscular development. Just very basic information may have provided for these women a necessary source of tolerance.

In reviewing these brutal cases, one is overcome with the seemingly flagrant disregard for human life sometimes expressed in situations combining, among other things, alcohol, sexual jealousy, and an oppressive lifestyle. One outstanding pattern that becomes evident from these police records has been documented generously in the literature: victim tolerance of mate battering as demonstrated by their remaining in such settings (see Browne, 1987, pp. 109–130). Consistent with findings from previous research (Gelles & Cornell, 1985, p. 36), these women, their children, and other family members, seemed to accept the situation as normal or at least tolerable. Even more disheartening is the suggestion that such violence may be perceived as a sign of love (Henton, Cate, Koval, Lloyd, & Christopher, 1983), and therefore perhaps even encouraged.

A valuable extension of this study would be the collection of in-depth interviews with homicidal women, eliciting from them the more personal dynamics of their violent behavior. The population should be taken from police records to include those women who avoid prosecution. It is these women who kill in a noncriminal way about whom we know so little. Their own retrospective interpretations of their violence and its antecedents would improve our understanding of the homicidal patterns outlined by this study. The data provided here call for relief from discrimination, unemployment, and poverty, perhaps through reform policies, but more likely through strategies revolutionary to our economic and social structures. In-depth accounts describing the interpersonal dynamics of these women's lives would help separate the influences of personality and of role structures. Perhaps adding traditional female role expectations to unemployment and poverty produces intolerable stress culminating in violence. Such a finding would not only have immediate implications for individual and family therapy, but for efforts to reform gender and family roles.

NOTES

1. Actually, 2 subjects are not arrestees; they were charged by the prosecuting attorney for felony killings, but were never taken into custody. For the purpose of this study, however, they are not distinguished from the arrestees.

2. The geographic grouping of states is that adopted by the U.S. Bureau of the Census.

3. In March of 1982, 70.3% of noninstitutionalized women and 54.9% of noninstitutionalized Blacks aged 25 and older in this country had completed 4 years of high school. In 1983, comparable proportions were 71.6% and 56.8% (U.S. Bureau of Census, 1984–1985).

4. This proportion is high when compared with the estimated 10.4% of Detroit residences reportedly having no telephone service in January of 1986 (Cross, personal communication, July, 1986).

5. Throughout this section data describing homicidal relationships characteristic of the sex-general 1982–1983 Detroit homicide popula-

tion refer not only to one-on-one killings, but also to multiple-offender and/or multiple-victim offenses. This means that the number of homicidal relationships associated with a certain analysis is greater than the number of actual homicides involved. The female research population data with which these sex-general data are compared include 136 offenders and 136 victims involved in 138 victim/offender relationships, including 2 double female offender/single victim and 2 single female offender/double victim incidents. Only female offenders are included in the analyses. The 21 male killers who were co-offenders in 14 of the homicidal incidents perpetrated by these women are excluded from these comparative analyses of demographic and social homicidal relationships.

6. Only those 2 studies utilized a coding scheme for hour of offense similar to that employed for the present study.

7. This estimate was computed by dividing the number of warrants issued by the Office of Wayne County Prosecuting Attorney in 1983 for murder and manslaughter in the city of Detroit (296) (B. Smith, personal communication, January, 1985) by the total number of 1983 arrests for murder and manslaughter recorded by the Homicide Section of the Detroit Department of Police (425); by then transforming that quotient (.696) to a percentage by multiplying by 100 (69.6%—this represents the proportion of arrestees who were issued warrants); and by subtracting that percentage from 100 (30.4%). The estimate is vulnerable to error in this and all subsequent studies to the extent that some arrestees may have died before the preliminary hearing or may have been issued a warrant for a crime other than murder or manslaughter. Those cases would be incorrectly counted as having been denied a warrant, artificially inflating the true proportion of dismissals.

Females as Victims and Offenders

Introduction to Part III

When compared with males, few females are involved in homicide as either victims or offenders. And when they are involved in either capacity, the fatal incident generally occurs in the context of either a domestic or familial relationship or both. Just over one-half of homicides perpetrated against females are mate-generated, as are around 60% of homicides committed by women. Perhaps these facts at least partially explain the research focus on mate-perpetrated homicide to the near exclusion of other fatal victim–offender relationships involving women.

Chapter 4, "Patterns of Marital Homicide: A Comparison of Husbands and Wives," documents the gender-specific patterned nature of homicide between spouses. Several productive replications have surfaced (Browne & Williams, 1993; Campbell, 1992a; Cazenave & Zahn, 1992; Mercy & Saltzman, 1989; Rasche, 1988; Silverman & Kennedy, 1993, pp. 70–76 [Canada]; Wilson & Daly, 1992), some skillfully extending and developing the theoretical underpinnings of marital homicide that inspired Sarah Fenstermaker and associates' (1983) critique, "the myth of mutual combat" in marital violence. This feminist perspective places spousal violence within the social-structural context of male domination and the subjection of women. It contends that while mate-perpetrated homicide against women typically is motivated by the desire of men to maintain the hierarchically gender-based

57

status quo, homicide involving male victims is likely to result from attempts on the part of women to alter or escape a threatening and intolerable patriarchal situation or system. My Detroit findings (Chapter 4) support this model, as do the results of most of the studies cited directly above. In the context of this feminist critique, Margo Wilson and Martin Daly (1992) elaborate the gendered, asymmetrical character of homicide between cross-gender relational partners:

> It is important to note that although U.S. women kill their husbands almost as often as the reverse (and in some groups, such as Chicago Blacks, even more often than the reverse), this does not imply symmetry in wives' and husbands' actions or motives. Men often hunt down and kill spouses who have left them; women hardly ever behave similarly. Men kill wives as part of planned murder-suicides; analogous acts by women are almost unheard of. Men kill in response to revelations of wifely infidelity; women almost never respond similarly, although their mates are more often adulterous. Men often kill wives after subjecting them to lengthy periods of coercive abuse and familicidal massacres, killing spouse and children together; women do not. Moreover, it seems clear that a large proportion of the spousal killings perpetrated by wives, but almost none of those perpetrated by husbands, are acts of self-defense. Unlike men, women kill male partners after years of suffering physical violence, after they have exhausted all available sources of assistance, when they feel trapped, and because they fear for their own lives. (p. 206)

It should be noted that there may exist distinct homicide patterns among the various types of cross-gender relational partnerships. Angela Browne and Kirk Williams (1993) report quite different patterns for married and unmarried couples; and my Detroit research suggests some differences between men who kill their mates (comprehensively defined) (Chapter 2) and men who kill specifically their wives (both legal and common-law) (Chapter 4). These findings indicate a clear need to examine patterned differences in the structure and process of homicide as it occurs among various categories of opposite-gender relational partnerships.

Part III is a study of contrast. While Chapter 4 examines women in their most common homicidal context, Chapter 5, "When Females Kill One Another: The Exceptional Case," observes them in their least. This female-on-female profile has enjoyed one replication—Mann's (1993b) thorough and insightful study of 57 cases drawn from police and court records of six major U.S. cities. While the two profiles are consistent in important ways, they demonstrate some interesting points of divergence (see Table 1 of Mann [1993b] for a variable-by-variable comparison of the Goetting and Mann profiles).

Patterns of Marital Homicide: A Comparison of Husbands and Wives

4

Most Americans view the family as a center for warmth, affection, acceptance, and happiness that serves as a refuge from the more competitive, stressful, and violent outside world. This image remains intact in spite of the fact that for over a decade now, research and the media have demonstrated the "underside" (Adler, 1981) of domestic life. It has become clear that the home is a dangerous place; more violence occurs there than outside its doors (Pagelow, 1984). Perhaps we cling to notions of the idealized family with good reason. Maybe the image of wise and devoted husbands and wives lovingly nurturing one another and their attractive, courteous, obedient, and charming children through the typical stages of the life cycle provides us with an important source of comfort (Pagelow, 1984). Or perhaps, as is suggested by Steinmetz and Straus (1974), this myth of domestic tranquility plays a critical role in the maintenance of the social institution of the family by encouraging individuals to marry, to stay married, and to have children. Whatever causes the persistence of this ideology, we should recognize that it may not occur without cost, for it likely has served to limit the objective analysis of family violence (Steinmetz & Straus, 1974). It is only through such analysis that we may become freed to understand and perhaps ultimately prevent such violence.

The purpose of this study is to contribute to the very limited data based on one form of family violence in the United States,

61

that is marital homicide, which involves the killing of a person by his or her spouse. In 1984 marital homicide accounted for nearly half of intrafamily homicide, making it the most frequent type of intrafamily victim-offender relationship (Straus, 1986). This research is intended to update sociological knowledge on the subject, and to extend current information by introducing additional variables. What remains the most important socio- logical inquiry into marital homicide, Wolfgang's (1956) Phila- delphia study, is now dated by over three decades. More recent efforts focus exclusively on homicidal wives (Browne, 1986, 1988; Bunyak, 1986; Mann, 1988; Totman, 1978). The concerns ad- dressed by this study relate to the general contextual nexus of marital homicide as well as to specific gender-based compari- sons. What kinds of people kill their spouses? When, where, and under what circumstance do they act? What weapons do they select? What motivational forces come into play? Is the fatal act typically offensive or defensive? Is alcohol involved? Are there witnesses? Does the offender flee the scene? What legal disposi- tions are associated with this behavior? Finally, do husbands and wives differ from one another on these factors? Wolfgang (1956) discovered gender to be a critical determinant of weapon selec- tion, room of offense, victim precipitation, and legal disposition. Do these correlates hold true in the 1990s in a different Midwest- ern city?

RESEARCH METHODS

The subjects selected for this study include the total popula- tion of 84 arrestees,[1] 28 male and 56 female,[2] accused of having killed their spouses (both legal and common-law) in the city of Detroit, Michigan, during 1982 and 1983 (except those attributed to the negligent use of a vehicle). The study is limited, again, by its lack of generalizability; its subjects are drawn from an urban, predominantly Black population with an inordinately high homi- cide rate. The 84 cases constituting this study population account for 11.2% of all closed homicide cases in that city during those two years. Data collection took place in June 1986 in the offices of the Homicide Section of the Detroit Police Department. Police-recorded information regarding each case, including the Investigator's Report, Interrogation Record, and Witness Statements, was electronically copied for subsequent perusal.

The data were tabulated and, when feasible, comparisons were made with the total population of Detroit arrestees for homicides committed during 1982 and 1983, and with previous homicide studies employing general populations and offenders. Since the proportion of homicide arrestees who are accused of having killed spouses remains between 8–9%, this means that the comparisons employed should have, according to the laws of probability, utilized populations and samples constituting approximately 91% members who are not offenders against spouses. Clearly the comparisons applied for this study are less than ideal on two counts: (1) the comparison groups are not totally mutually exclusive (i.e., the other-than-offender-against-spouse groups actually contain some offenders against spouses); and (2) except when 1982 and 1983 Detroit data are available, the comparison groups are not geographically and temporally comparable. Throughout the analyses, notable differences between male and female subjects are acknowledged. Population characteristics and gender differences are summarized in Table 4.1.

The information reported herein is presented through use of a 3-part organizational scheme: demographic and social characteristics of offenders and victims, circumstances of offense, and arrest disposition.

ANALYSES

Demographic and Social Characteristics of Offenders and Victims

Race. Research repeatedly has verified that homicide offenders and their victims in the United States are disproportionately Black. Detroit provides no exception to this generalization, and

TABLE 4.1 Summary of Population and Subpopulation (by Gender) Characteristics

Characteristics	(Sub) Population Size[1]	Number	Percent	Mean
Demographic and Social Characteristics				
Offender: Black	84	76	90.5	
Women	56	54	96.4	
Men	28	22	78.6	
Victim: Black	84	77	91.7	
Women	28	22	78.6	
Men	56	55	98.2	
Offender: Age	84			35.5 years
Women	56			34.1 years
Men	28			38.3 years
Victim: Age	84			37.9 years
Women	28			34.8 years
Men	56			39.4 years
Offender: Lived in family setting	80	76	95.0	
Women	54	52	96.3	
Men	26	24	92.3	
Offender: Residing with spouse	84	73	86.9	
Women	56	51	91.1	
Men	28	22	78.6	
Offender: Child(ren)	73	59	80.8	
Women	53	43	81.1	
Men	20	16	80.0	
Offender: Completed 12 years school	63	33	52.4	
Women	45	22	48.9	
Men	18	11	61.1	
Offender: Unemployed	72	53	73.6	
Women	50	39	78.0	
Men	22	14	63.6	
Offender: Welfare recipient	33	22	66.7	
Women	28	20	71.4	
Men	5	2	40.0	
Offender: No residential telephone	74	18	24.3	
Women	52	14	26.9	
Men	22	4	18.2	
Offender: Arrest record	53	30	56.6	
Women	35	18	51.4	
Men	18	12	66.7	
Circumstances of Offense				
Motive: Domestic discord	84	79	94.0	
Women (O)[2]	56	53	94.6	
Men (O)	28	26	92.9	
Method: Gunshot	84	49	58.3	
Women (V)[3]	28	18	64.3	
Men (V)	56	31	55.4	
Method: Stabbing	84	27	32.1	
Women (V)	28	4	14.3	
Men (V)	56	23	41.1	

TABLE 4.1 (Continued)

Characteristics	(Sub)Population Size[1]	Number	Percent	Mean
Single-victim/Single-offender	84	81	96.4	
Women (O)	56	55	98.2	
Men (O)	28	26	92.9	
Victim precipitation	55	33	60.0	
Women (O)	45	32	71.1	
Men (O)	10	1	10.0	
Location: Residence	84	75	89.3	
Women (O)	56	51	91.1	
Men (O)	28	24	85.7	
Location: Bedroom	69	27	39.1	
Women (O)	49	15	30.6	
Men (O)	20	12	60.0	
Time: Weekend	82	49	59.7	
Women (O)	56	34	60.7	
Men (O)	26	15	57.7	
Time: 8 P.M.–1:59 A.M.	81	34	42.0	
Women (O)	55	25	45.5	
Men (O)	26	9	34.6	
Offender: Alcohol	31	27	87.1	
Women	21	18	85.7	
Men	10	9	90.0	
Victim: Alcohol	33	31	93.9	
Women	26	25	96.2	
Men	7	6	85.7	
Audience	82	32	39.0	
Women (O)	55	23	41.8	
Men (O)	27	9	33.3	
Fled scene	77	21	27.3	
Women	51	8	15.7	
Men	26	13	50.0	
Arrest Disposition				
Denied warrant	78[3]	23	29.5	
Women	54[3]	20	37.0	
Men	24[3]	3	12.5	
Convicted of murder or manslaughter	53[4]	33	62.3	
Women	34[4]	16	47.1	
Men	19[4]	17	89.4	
Prison sentences	38[5]	27	71.1	
Women	21[5]	12	57.1	
Men	17[5]	15	88.2	

1. Number of subjects for which information was available
2. O = offenders; V = victims
3. Number of subjects at risk of prosecution
4. Number of subjects processed by court
5. Number of subjects convicted

neither do the men and women who kill their spouses in that city. In 1980, 63% of the Detroit population was Black (U.S. Bureau of the Census, 1984–85). Information on the offenders against spouses in that population indicated that 90.5% (76) of them and 91.7% (77) of their victims were of that racial category. Three of the offenses under observation here were interracial: In two cases a White woman killed her Black husband, and in the remaining case a Black woman killed her White husband.

Age. The study population of offenders ranged in age between 18 and 82 years, with a mean of 35.5. Their victims showed approximately the same age range, with a mean of 37.9 years of age. As might be expected, the victims of the women generally were older than they, while the victims of the men generally were younger than their slayers. The killers and victims under observation here were slightly older than the general population of arrested killers and slain victims in Detroit during 1982 and 1983. Those mean arrestee and victim ages were 31.5 and 35 years, respectively.

Residential Mode and Parental Status of Offender. Nearly all (95%, or 76) of the 80 killers who reported residential mode were living in a family setting; all except 11 (86.9%) of the total population were residing with their victimized spouses at the time of the offense. Nearly 81% (59) of the 73 offenders for whom data were available acknowledged at least one living child.

Social Class Indicators of Offender. Just over half of the 63 offenders for whom information on formal education was available had completed at least twelve years of school. Over 20% (13) were educated beyond that level. These data reflect a relatively low level of formal education when compared with the general United States population at the same point in time.[3] Employment information was available for 72 of the arrestees; nearly three-quarters (73.6%, or 53) of whom were unemployed, one of them having retired and another currently collecting disability compensation.

These data on education and unemployment, in conjunction with the facts that two-thirds (22) of the 33 subjects for whom information was available were welfare recipients, and 24.3% (18) of the 74 for whom data were recorded reported having no residential telephone,[4] are congruent with other studies suggesting that homicide offenders are concentrated in the lower social classes (Bensing, Schroeder, & Jackson, 1960; Swigert & Farrell, 1978; Wolfgang, 1958).

Arrest Record of Offender. Homicide records indicate that 56.6% (30) of the 53 offenders for whom data were available had been arrested at least once prior to the offenses that precipitated them into the study population. While this is a crude measure of criminal history, since it fails to delineate the particular charges and dispositions associated with arrests, it does suggest that a high proportion of the spouse killers under observation here are likely to have had criminal backgrounds. Available research indicates a basic consistency when comparing this particular category of offender with general populations of homicide offenders on this dimension. Wolfgang (1958) reports 64% and Swigert and Farrell (1978) report 56% of their homicide offender populations as having had previous arrests.

Circumstances of Offense

Homicidal Motive. Most marital homicides occur in the context of domestic discord. The typical scenario involves an argument or a physical or verbal confrontation, perhaps over sexual indiscretion, money, or the threat of terminating the relationship. In such cases, the death blow usually is the culminating event in a long history of interpersonal tensions entrenched in violence. It is struck in the urgency of passionate anger; the fatal outcome commonly is realized with shock and disbelief. Often the offender had not intended to go so far. Homicidal marriages appear to be strongly ambivalent in nature, and the deadly act seems to dissipate hateful sentiments on the part of the offender, leaving a sense of despair at the loss of a loved one (Browne, 1987).

All but five (94%) of the cases under consideration here conform to this general description. One exception involved a woman who beat her husband to death with a baseball bat as he was beating their son. Two other cases were premeditated and motivated by insurance benefits. In one such case, a 40-year-old woman and her 18-year-old boyfriend conspired to kill her 29-year-old husband for the freedom to have a baby together as well as for insurance benefits. The boyfriend beat the husband to death with a baseball bat, arranging the scene to appear as though the death had resulted from a drug-related robbery. She was convicted of manslaughter, and he of first degree murder; both were sentenced to prison. In the other premeditated incident, a 26-year-old woman beat and shot to death her estranged husband of the same age after having secured several insurance policies on his life without his knowledge. Three months before the fatal incident, the offender had commented to her mother and sisters that she was going to make them rich, and that she planned to buy a Mercedes Benz. Though at the wake she had to be pulled away from the coffin as she exclaimed, "All I want to do is tell him that I was sorry to do it," she never formally admitted her guilt, and was acquitted. Finally, two exceptional cases were accidental shootings.

Homicidal Method. Firearms are the most common means of inflicting death in this country. Between 1968 and 1978 the proportion of homicides committed with firearms varied between 63–65.7% (Riedel, Zahn, & Mock, 1985). In Detroit during 1982 and 1983, 65.8% of the 1138 reported homicides were shootings. Another 17.8% were stabbings, 11.4% were beatings, 0.7% were burnings, and 4.2% were conducted by some other means. The distribution of homicidal methods associated with the victims of marital homicide in Detroit during those years differs from that associated with the general population of victims primarily in that a somewhat lower proportion of the spouses (58.3%, or 49) died of gunshot wounds, and a much higher proportion (32.1%, or 27) were stabbed. Five victims (5.6%) were beaten to death, 3 (3.6%) with blunt instruments, and 2 (2.4%) through the use of hands and/or feet as weapons; and another 3 (3.6%) were strangled or suffocated. Distributions of methods vary distinctly by gender. A somewhat lower proportion of husbands than wives died of gunshot wounds, and a much higher proportion (nearly triple) were stabbed. This is consistent with Wolfgang's (1956) observation that wives were more than twice as likely as husbands to use cutting instruments, attributing that difference to "cultural tradition": Because of their domestic role (i.e., involving food preparation), women are more accustomed to using knives than are men (Wolfgang, 1958). Additionally, all beatings using hand and/or feet and all strangulations or suffocations were inflicted on wives.

Number of Victims and Offenders. Almost all homicides are one-on-one incidents, with a higher concentration among domestic killings. Detroit provides no exception to this generalization, and neither do the men and women who kill their spouses in that city. In Detroit during 1982 and 1983, 87.9% of the 578 homicides for which information is available involved a single victim and a single offender. Another 10.6% of those offenses were single-victim/multiple offender; 1.4% of those offenses were multiple-victim/single offender; and the remaining .2% were multiple-victim/multiple offender. All except 3 (96.4%) of the homicides against spouses occurring in that city during those years were one-on-one. Two of the exceptional incidents, both perpetrated by men, involved a single offender, one with two victims (a wife and their 18-year-old daughter), and the other with three (a common-law wife, her 10-year-old son, and their 8-year-old son). The third case involved the woman and her boyfriend who conspired to kill her husband for insurance benefits.

Victim Precipitation. Information on victim precipitation could be gleaned from 1982 and 1983 Detroit police records for 55 homicides perpetrated against spouses. Sixty percent (33) of these cases were victim precipitated. This proportion is high when

compared with data from studies of general homicide populations, which report victim precipitation to characterize between
22 and 37.9% of deadly encounters (Curtis, 1974; Voss &
Hepburn, 1968; Wolfgang, 1958). This discrepancy can be explained by the predominance of homicidal wives in the study
population (45 of the 55 subjects for whom information was
available were wives). It has been established that a relatively high
proportion of spousal homicides perpetrated by women are victim precipitated (Wolfgang, 1956; Wilbanks, 1983b), and the
wives under observation here conform to that generalization
(71.1% of their offenses were of that nature).

Spatial Considerations. Marital homicides are far more likely
to occur in the private residence setting than are the general
population of homicides. Over 89% (75) of the killings in this
study were accomplished in a home: 78.6% (66) occurred at the
common residence of the offender and victim, 8.3% (7) at the
residence of the offender, 1.2% (1) at the residence of the victim
and another 1.2% (1) at the residence of a friend. Additionally,
8 offenses (9.5%) took place on public streets, and one (1.2%) at
the place of business of the victim.

Over 39% (27) of the 69 offenses committed at a private residence for which information was available occurred in a bedroom; again, this closely approximates the 35% reported by Wolfgang (1956). Another 21.7% (15) took place in the living room.
Approximately 10% (7) occurred outside the actual residence
(usually on the porch or in the yard) and in the kitchen, 7.2% (5)
in the dining room, 4.3% (3) in a hallway, 2.9% (2) each in a
bathroom and an "other" room, and 1.4% (1) in the basement.
Like the husbands observed in the Wolfgang (1956) study, those
under observation here were twice as likely to kill in a bedroom
as were the wives. Only 1 of the 6 offenses occurring in the kitchen
was perpetrated by a husband, and all 7 of the outdoor incidents
were perpetrated by wives.

Temporal Considerations. Except for a moderate increase
during January and February, the marital homicides in Detroit

during those years displayed no apparent seasonal fluctuations. Their frequencies over the ten or perhaps twelve months appear to be randomly distributed, with a high of 13.1% in January to a low of 4.8% in May and October.

Relative to days of week, the research population of marital homicides conformed closely to the norm. Data are consistent in indicating that homicide is concentrated during weekends, peaking on Saturdays (Bensing, Schroeder, & Jackson, 1960; Voss & Hepburn, 1968; Wolfgang, 1958), and these husbands and wives provide no exception to that generalization. Nearly 60% (49) of the 82 killings in this study for which information was available occurred on Fridays, Saturdays, and Sundays (the days of the 3 highest frequencies), which clearly is in line with the range extending between 56.6%–84% reported by studies using general populations of offenders. The subjects conformed less closely to hourly norms. Wolfgang (1958) and Pokorney (1986) provide the only two sources of information on homicide that effectively can be compared with data describing the Detroit killers on the subject of time of offense.[5] The two studies are consistent with one another in indicating that approximately half of homicides occur between 8:00 P.M. and 1:59 A.M., and another quarter occur between 2:00 P.M. and 7:59 P.M. Basically congruous with these general homicide populations, the spouses under observation here executed 42% (34) of the 81 homicides for which information was available between 8:00 P.M. and 1:59 A.M., and 28.4% (23) between 2:00 P.M. and 7:59 P.M. The remaining 29.6% (24) of the cases apparently were evenly distributed throughout the remaining hours of the day.

Alcohol Consumption. Available information suggests that alcohol consumption contributes to the homicide drama (Collins, 1981; Wolfgang, 1958; MacDonald, 1961; Riedel, Zahn, & Mock, 1985; Wolfgang, 1958) and to marital violence (Frieze & Browne, 1989; Leonard & Jacob, 1988). The information gleaned from witness statements for this study of homicidal spouses is limited in that data were available for just over a third of the subjects. But these data suggest that alcohol may have played a vital role

in many of the incidents. At least 32.1% (27) of the total population of offenders had been drinking prior to the homicide, as had
at least 36.9% (31) of their victims.

Audience and Offender's Response. Thirty-nine percent (32)
of the 82 victims for whom data were recorded received their fatal
blows before witnesses. Most (67.5%, or 52) of the 77 offenders
for whom information was available remained at the homicide
scene until investigators arrived; only 27.3% (21) fled to avoid
detection. Another four (5.2%), all men, committed suicide at the
scene. This gender differential relating to suicide among spouse-
killers is consistent with other research (Daly & Wilson, 1988).
Furthermore, it is interesting to note that more than three times
the proportion of men than women fled the scene.

Arrest Disposition

Prosecuting Attorney. Of the 78 spouse killers for whom information was available who were at risk of prosecution (excluding the 4 suicides), 29.5% (23) were denied warrant for criminal
charge by the prosecutor. This proportion is congruent with the
estimated 30.4% of the general population of homicide arrestees
for that city during 1983 who enjoyed similar denial,[6] suggesting an absence of prosecutorial bias toward this category of offender. Nearly three times the proportion of women as men who
were at risk were denied warrant, which is not surprising in light
of the fact that such a high proportion of incidents perpetrated
by women were victim precipitated. Additionally, the notion of
chivalry may enter in here; most studies of felony defendants have
found that women are more likely to be released prior to trial
than are their male counterparts (Gruhl, Welch, & Spohn 1984).

Court. Court dispositions associated with the 53 arrestees who
were processed by the Court (excluding the subject never taken
into custody, the four suicides, and one subject who skipped
bond) indicate that 62.3% (33) were convicted of a misdemeanor

including Careless Discharge, Intentionally Pointing a Firearm Without Malice, and Careless and Reckless Use of a Firearm: Death Resulting (high misdemeanor); and 28.3% (15) were acquitted. Of the 38 convicted arrestees, 71.1% (27) received prison sentences: three for life, and the rest for a mean minimum of 7.7 years. A total of 26 of the 33 convicted of Murder or Manslaughter (78.8%) were sentenced to incarceration. One woman convicted of a misdemeanor received a prison sentence of fifteen days. Again, with court disposition, leniency toward women is suggested. Consistent with the observations of Wolfgang (1956), a much lower proportion of women than men who were processed by the court were convicted of Murder or Manslaughter. Also, a much lower proportion of convicted women were sentenced to incarceration. This apparent leniency directed toward women by the court system is incongruent with the discrimination applied to them as described by Browne (1988).

DISCUSSION

The construction of a statistical profile describing the population of 84 men and women arrested for killing their spouses in the predominantly Black city of Detroit, Michigan, during 1982 and 1983 yields the image of a Black man or woman in his or her middle thirties who lives in a family setting. He or she is an undereducated, unemployed parent with an arrest record, whose finale in a series of heated arguments or confrontations with his or her spouse culminated in a defensive fatal gunshot in a bedroom or the living room of their residence on a weekend.

The findings reported herein are totally consistent with those derived from Wolfgang's (1956) Philadelphia study conducted over thirty years ago. This fact suggests that a robust and predictable pattern of circumstances surrounds marital homicide. It also verifies that the marital homicide experience differs significantly by gender: For the homicidal husband the act is nearly always offensive; for the wife it is usually defensive. This supports the popular contention that marital homicide, regardless of who inflicts the fatal blow, typically is a reflection of wife abuse (Browne, 1986; Mann, 1988; "Wives Face Bigger Risk," 1989). In the words of Russell (1982): "The statistics on the murder of husbands, along with the statistics on the murder of wives, are both indicators of the desperate plight of some wives, not a sign that in this one area, males and females are equally violent" (p. 299). Previous research indicates that homicide does not occur without warning—nonlethal violence precedes domestic homicide (Straus, 1986). Abused women have been warned, yet they remain in a violent situation hoping for improvement. Consistent with other studies (Gelles & Cornell, 1985), the wives involved here along with witnesses to the incidents, usually children and other family members, seemingly accepted the situation as normal or at least tolerable. Even more disheartening is the suggestion that such violence inflicted in the context of a romantic relationship is in some cases perceived as a sign of love (Henton et al., 1983), and therefore perhaps even encouraged of the participants by one another.

Clearly there is a critical need for effective intervention and support agencies to accommodate the needs of women victimized by domestic violence. Help must be provided to prevent the kinds of fatal incidents depicted in this study. Police should be trained specifically in domestic concerns, and urged to view reported cases of domestic conflict in a more serious light (Pagelow, 1984). Additionally, it is believed by some that they need to respond more effectively (Elliott, 1989; Gelles & Straus, 1989; Gillespie, 1989).

Available evidence suggests that continued domestic violence against women may be reduced by police arrests (Sherman & Berk, 1984). Langen and Innes's (1986) Analysis of National Crime Survey (NCS) data indicate that simply reporting such violence may decrease the likelihood and severity of subsequent assaults. Only an estimated 14.4% of incidents of domestic violence against women are brought to police attention (Kantor, Kaufman, & Straus, 1987). The most common reason offered by 1978 through 1982 NCS female respondents for not reporting domestic violence was that the woman considered the incident a private or personal matter (Langen & Innes, 1986). These women need to be dissuaded from that perspective, and encouraged to seek formal intervention.

NOTES

1. Actually, five subjects are not arrestees: One was charged by the prosecuting attorney for a felony killing, but was never taken into custody, and four others committed suicide at the scene. For the purpose of this study, however, these five offenders are not distinguished from the arrestees.

2. This finding of a relatively high proportion of wife/husband versus husband/wife homicides among this predominantly Black population is consistent with the results of three studies (Block, 1985; Plass & Straus, 1987; "Wives Face Bigger Risk," 1989) that discovered a higher number of female than male spouse killers among Blacks, but a lower number among Whites (and in Block's study, Latin Americans). Plass and Straus suggest that White women, because of greater economic and social-emotional dependency on their husbands, may be more vulnerable to being victims of wife beating—and homicide—than are Black women.

3. In March 1982, 70.9% of the noninstitutionalized United States population aged 25 and older had completed four years of high school. In 1983 that proportion increased to 72.1% (U.S. Bureau of the Census, 1984–85).

4. This proportion is high when compared with the estimated 10.4% of Detroit residences reportedly having no telephone service in January 1986 (Cross, 1986).

5. Only those two studies utilized a coding scheme for hour of offense similar to that employed for the present study.

6. This estimate was computed by dividing the number of warrants issued by the Office of Wayne County Prosecuting Attorney in 1983 for murder and manslaughter in the city of Detroit (296) (Smith, 1985) by the total number of 1983 arrests for murder and manslaughter recorded by the Homicide Section of the Detroit Department of Police (425); by then transforming that quotient (.696) to a percentage by multiplying by 100 (69.6%—this represents the proportion of arrestees who were

issued warrants); and by subtracting that percentage from 100 (30.4%). The estimate is vulnerable to error to the extent that some arrestees may have died before the preliminary hearing or may have been issued a warrant for a crime other than murder or manslaughter. Those cases would be incorrectly counted as having been denied a warrant, artificially inflating the true proportion of dismissals.

When Females Kill One Another: The Exceptional Case

5

Deborah was a 22-year-old unmarried and unemployed Black woman with one child and a tenth-grade education. Early one Wednesday evening in June, Deborah and her two sisters, Geneva, 30, and Brenda, 22, were sitting around the dining room table at Deborah's home, drinking beer and talking. The discussion led to an argument and ultimately a fight between Deborah and Geneva over a conversation that Deborah had had with Geneva's boyfriend. During the fight a television set was broken, curtains were pulled down, and other furniture was destroyed. At one point Brenda stopped the fight, but it was resumed and eventually made its way to the front porch, where Deborah stabbed Geneva in the back with a small butcher knife from the kitchen. Geneva died there on the grass of multiple stab wounds. Deborah was arrested at the scene, stating that she didn't mean to do it. Six months later she was acquitted by a jury.

Sandra was an obese and unattractive 40-year-old unemployed White woman who lived with her two children. She had a high school education. On a Wednesday just before Christmas, Sandra spent the day drinking in a bar with her former husband (married seven years, one child), Clarence, who owned the bar, and his girlfriend of six months, Georgia. Sometime during the afternoon the two women argued about Clarence and the bar. Georgia snapped to Sandra that Sandra could have Clarence back, to which Sandra retorted that she didn't want him. Sandra left the bar for home, got her twenty-gauge semiautomatic shotgun, and returned to the bar, leaving the loaded gun outside in her car. The argument with Georgia escalated. Sandra went out to her car, got the weapon, and returned to the back door of the bar and knocked. When Georgia answered the door, she was killed with a single shot. When Clarence rushed to the scene from inside the bar, he was killed in the same manner. Sandra then drove home, hid the gun in a neighbor's yard, and went to the residence of her boyfriend to sleep until police came to arrest her that night. Sandra was sentenced to 50 to 75 years in Jackson State Prison.

Jeanetta was a 39-year-old Black former mental patient with an eleventh-grade education who resided with her minister husband, Cleaver, and her two small children. The older child, Marietta, was 5 years old, and the product of a former marriage. Early one Sunday morning in May, Marietta was beaten to death by Jeanetta and Cleaver. At the time of death, the child's body was covered with bruises and welts. There was a cut on her head, puncture wounds on her arm and shoulder, and her buttocks were extremely swollen. Also, her front teeth had been knocked out. Jeanetta later explained that, in addition to Cleaver's beatings, she beat the child usually daily with a curtain rod, belt, or tape recorder cord, and that during the previous day she had pushed Marietta under water for two minutes several times "to show her that I was bigger than her and so that she would mind me." Police investigation uncovered a long history of maternal neglect and abuse toward Marietta. Both Jeanetta and Cleaver were sentenced to 10 to 15 years in Jackson State Prison.

These cases describe 3 of the 15 women who are reported to have killed another female in a predominantly Black Midwestern city during 1982 and 1983. Relatively few homicides in this country are perpetrated by females—between 13% and 14%—and when females do kill, they nearly always do so across gender lines. Between 1981 and 1985 the proportion of female homicide arrestees in the United States accused of having killed a male ranged between 81% and 85%. It becomes apparent, then, that female-on-female homicide is a rare form of patterned behavior.

The purpose of this chapter is to explore the circumstances surrounding this unusual type of deviance that has been totally ignored by the scholarly community. Under what conditions do women kill members of their own gender? What kinds of people are these women and their female victims, and how were they related to one another before the deadly incident that predisposed them to this study population?

The subjects selected for this research include the total population of 15 female arrestees[1] associated with intrasex homicides (except those attributed to the negligent use of a vehicle) committed in the city of Detroit, Michigan, during 1982 and 1983 and their 16 female victims. The perpetrators constitute a subpopulation of a broader research base consisting of all 136 female arrestees for homicide in that city during those years (see Goetting, 1988b, for an analysis of those base data). Data collection took place in June of 1986 in the offices of the Homicide section of the Detroit Police Department. Police-recorded information regarding each case, including the Investigator's Report, Interrogation Record, and Witness Statements was electronically copied for subsequent perusal. The quantity and quality of information describing these 15 women varies enormously. Some case folders bulged with a multiplicity of richly detailed witness accounts, while others left specifics to the imagination.

THE OFFENDERS

The offenders ranged in age between 19 and 45 years, having a mean of 29.9 years and a standard deviation of 7.4 years. Eleven (73.3%) were Black, and the remaining four (26.7%) were White. Of the 7 women for whom data were recorded (85.7%), 6 were Protestant; the other claimed no religious affiliation. All subjects were residents of Detroit. Of the 11 for whom information was reported, 9 (81.9%) had originated in the North Central portion of the United States,[2] all but two of them in Detroit. Over half (53.3% or 8) of these female perpetrators were married and living with their husband, and all 14 for whom data were available had children, usually one or two. All 13 for whom information was reported were living with their family or lover at the time of the incident. Approximately 61% (8) of the 13 offenders for whom data were recorded had completed four years of high school; 1 had achieved more formal schooling.[3] Nearly three-quarters (10) of the 14 subjects for whom data were available were unemployed at the time of the killing, and 57.1% (4) of the 7 for whom information was reported were recipients of welfare. This information on education, unemployment, and welfare status, in conjunction with the fact that 30.8% (4) of the 13 subjects for whom data were available reported having no residential telephone,[4] is congruent with other studies suggesting that homicide offenders are concentrated in the lower social classes (Bensing, Schroeder, & Jackson, 1960, pp. 128–29; Swigert & Farrell, 1978, p. 193; Wolfgang, 1958, pp. 36–39). Information on previous arrests indicates that 5 of the 10 women for whom data were available had been arrested previously.

THE VICTIMS AND CIRCUMSTANCES

In total, 9 adults and 7 young children (under the age of 6 years) were killed in the 15 incidents under the following circumstances:

- 2 (twin) infants died of neglect (starvation) in custody of their mother who was declared insane;
- 1 child was beaten by her adoptive mother;
- 2 children were beaten by their mothers and stepfathers (Jeanetta);
- 2 children were beaten by their stepmothers; in one case the father was a co-offender;
- 1 woman was shot by her boyfriend's former wife in the context of a quarrel (Sandra);
- 1 woman was stabbed by her former boyfriend's common-law wife in the context of a quarrel;
- 2 women were killed (one shot, one stabbed) by lesbian lovers in the context of domestic quarrels;

1 elderly woman was stabbed by her daughter who was declared insane;

1 woman was stabbed by her sister in the context of a quarrel (Deborah);

1 woman was stabbed in self-defense by her niece in the context of a quarrel;

1 woman was shot by her estranged neighbor while forcing her way into the neighbor's apartment to retrieve loaned clothing; and

1 woman was stabbed by an acquaintance in the context of a quarrel.

The victims ranged in age from 21 months to 66 years, with a mean of 21.4 years and a standard deviation of 19.5 years. Most (62.5% or 10) of them were younger than their killers, though 5 (31.3%) were older, and 1 (6.3%) was the same age. The mean difference in age between victim and offender was 18.3 years. Three-quarters (12) of the victims were Black, and the remaining 4 (25%) were White. All of the homicidal relationships under observation here were intraracial. All victims, like their assailants, were Detroit residents, and 10 (62.5%) lived with the perpetrator at the time of the incident.

Only 3 of the homicidal relationships (20%) were what Wolfgang (1958, p. 252) refers to as "victim precipitated"—those offenses in which the victim is the first in the homicide drama to use physical force directed against his or her subsequent slayer. This proportion is low when compared with data from studies of general homicide populations, which report victim precipitation to characterize between 22% and 37.9% of deadly encounters (Curtis, 1974, p. 83; Voss & Hepburn, 1968, p. 506; Wolfgang, 1958, p. 254). The proportion is even lower when compared with the 55% found to be associated with the base population from which this subpopulation was drawn, women who kill. This low incidence of victim precipitation among these women who had killed other females can be explained by the high proportion of victims who were young children (43.8%) and therefore not at risk of imposing serious physical force against an adult.

Most homicides are one-on-one incidents, and this population of female offenders provides no exception to that generalization. Two-thirds (10) of these subjects acted alone toward a single victim. In total, 2 of the women perpetrated double killings: in one case a set of infant twin daughters was allowed to starve, and in the other (Sandra), a former husband and his girlfriend were shot in a bar. Additionally, in 3 cases (20%), all instances of child abuse, the perpetrator acted with a co-offender, all 3 being her husband.

In total, 6 of the 14 offenders for whom information was available (42.9%) displayed their destructive behavior in view of at least one witness. This proportion is somewhat lower than the 54.4% found in the 1978 Swigert and Farrell study (Felson & Steadman, 1983, p. 73). Of the 6 deadly incidents, 2 occurred in the context of group recreation—one in a bar (Sandra), and the other (involving lesbian lovers) at a social gathering of family and friends. In another case (Deborah), a woman stabbed her sister in the presence of another sister. The remaining 3 incidents were observed by children. The woman who stabbed her aunt was witnessed by four or five family members, including her 3-year-old son; and 2 small children were beaten to death in full view of their four siblings in one case, and a step-sibling in the other case.

All but one of the killings under scrutiny here were executed in a private residence; the exception (Sandra) took place in a bar. The distribution of incidents over the months of the year indicates a slight increase during December–January, and a somewhat more discernible increase during March–April. Half of the 14 victims for whom date of expiration could be calculated (the twins were starved over a period of many days, and their date(s) of expiration remain(s) undetermined) died on a Saturday (4) or Sunday (3). This proportion is congruent with other research (Bensing et al., 1960, p. 11; Voss & Hepburn, 1968, p. 504; Wolfgang, 1958, p. 107) indicating that homicide is concentrated during weekends, peaking on Saturdays. Also consistent with previous studies (Pokorney, 1965, p. 482; Wolfgang, 1958, p. 108), half of the 12 victims for whom information was available died between 8:00 P.M. and 1:59 A.M., and another quarter between

2:00 P.M. and 7:59 P.M. Clearly there is a temporal order inherent in homicide to which this study population conforms.

Most of the offenders under observation here remained at the homicide scene or with the victim until investigators arrived; only 20% (3) fled to avoid detection.

ARREST AND COURT DISPOSITIONS

In total, 20% (3) of the offenders in this study were denied warrant by the prosecuting attorney. This is low when compared with the estimated 30.4% of the general population of Detroit homicide arrestees during 1983 who were similarly denied warrant,[5] and even lower when compared with the 36.4% associated with the base population of female perpetrators from which this study population was drawn. Further analysis controlling for severity of crime and other factors are necessary in order to pursue properly the question of prosecutoral bias applied to this category of homicide offenders.

Court dispositions relating to the 11 arrestees not denied warrant by the prosecuting attorney (this is excluding the subject who was charged but never arrested) indicate that 81.8% (9) were convicted of a felony killing, and the remaining 18.2% (2) were acquitted. Of the 9 convicted arrestees, 8 (88.9%) received prison sentences—one for life, and the rest for a mean minimum sentence of 11.57 years with a standard deviation of 17.3 years. The one convicted arrestee who was not given a prison sentence was the mother who allowed her twins to starve to death. She was judged insane before a Recorder's Court and sentenced to five years probation plus court costs.

CONCLUSION

The construction of a statistical profile describing the population of 15 females arrested for killing other females in the predominantly Black city of Detroit, Michigan, during 1982 and 1983 yields the image of a locally born, Black, 30-year-old Detroit mother who is Protestant, married, and living with her family. She is an undereducated, unemployed, welfare recipient with an arrest record, who kills an intimate associate, often a child, in the passion of anger in a private residence on a weekend between 8:00 P.M. and 1:59 A.M.

Upon examination of this rare form of homicide where women victimize members of their own gender, one is struck by one outstanding observation: the high proportion of victims who are small children. We know now that few homicides are perpetrated by women, and that when a woman does kill, the act typically occurs in the context of the final in a series of heated arguments or fights with her current or former husband or lover (Goetting, 1988a). But when women kill other females, as suggested by this one study population, nearly half of their victims are their children or stepchildren.

What emerges through careful inspection of the police documents describing these 15 female killers again and again is the portrayal of a person disadvantaged along multiple dimensions, and in many ways isolated from mainstream culture. These are minority mothers who, for the most part, are living in loosely structured relationships with men, and are poorly equipped to overcome the daily mundane struggles to just get by. They are drastically limited in the educational and occupational resources and in the social skills required to maintain a life of comfort and dignity in the United States today. Though their knowledge of the street scene is particularly keen, they are shrouded in ignorance in other areas critical to their sense of well-being. An example of such ignorance was a precipitating factor in one of the deadly incidents included in this study. A woman who beat to death her small daughter, argued convincingly that the child had *refused* to mind by continuing to dirty her pants in spite of constant reprimands. Such behavior on the part of the child was attributed to willful lack of compliance, to stubbornness deserving of punitive sanction. It seems clear that this woman failed to understand that in the early years of life, a child's psychomuscular constitution may not yet be fully developed to control eliminative functions. Just that very piece of knowledge may have lightened the burden of parenthood significantly for this woman, providing a source of tolerance necessary to the vitality of the parent–child relationship.

A valuable extension of this study would be the collection of in-depth interviews with women who have killed females, eliciting from them the more personal dynamics of their violent behavior. The subjects, like those studied herein, should be taken from police records to include those who avoid prosecution. In an effort to better represent the national scene (Detroit represents an urban, predominantly Black population with an inordinately high homicide rate), subjects from a variety of geographic locations should be included. So that more confidence can be placed in the results, much higher numbers of subjects than the 15 offenders and 16 victims included here would be desirable. In-depth accounts describing the interpersonal dynamics of these women's lives would shed light on the antecedents to their violence—those rooted in personality as well as role structures.

NOTES

1. Actually, one subject is not an arrestee; she was charged by the prosecuting attorney for a felony killing, but was never taken into custody. For the purpose of this study, however, she is not distinguished from the arrestees.

2. Using the geographic grouping of states adopted by the U.S. Bureau of the Census, the North Central region includes Ohio, Indiana, Illinois, Michigan, Wisconsin, Minnesota, Iowa, Missouri, North Dakota, South Dakota, Nebraska, and Kansas.

3. These figures reflect a somewhat depressed level of formal education when compared with the general population of United States women at the same point in time. In March of 1982, 70.3% of non-institutionalized women aged 25 and older in this country had completed four years of high school. In 1983, the proportion had increased to 71.6% (U.S. Bureau of Census, 1984–1985).

4. This proportion is high when compared with the estimated 10.4% of Detroit residences reportedly having no telephone service in January of 1986 (C. Cross, Media Relations Manager, Michigan Bell Telephone Company, Detroit, Michigan, July 1986).

5. This estimate was computed by dividing the number of warrants issued by the Office of Wayne County Prosecuting Attorney in 1983 for murder and manslaughter in the city of Detroit (296) (B. Smith, Assistant Administrator, Office of Wayne County Prosecuting Attorney, telephone communication, January 17, 1985) by the total number of 1983 arrests for murder and manslaughter recorded by the Homicide Section of Detroit Department of Police (425); by then transforming that quotient (.696) to a percentage by multiplying by 100 (69.6%—this represents the proportion of arrestees who were issued warrants); and by subtracting that percentage from 100 (30.4%).

Child Victims

IV

Introduction to Part IV

The first of the two chapters in this section, "Child Victims of Homicide: A Portrait of Their Killers and the Circumstances of Their Deaths" (Chapter 6), provides a comprehensive profile of homicides against children under the age of 15. This particular chapter reflects a professional and personal-political interest as expressed in my keynote address to the 1993 Hartman National Conference on Children and their Families entitled "Do Americans Really Like Children?" (Goetting, 1994). That speech provides an extensive list of national-level indicators that the U.S., to its own detriment and out of lack of political will to correct the situation, is neglecting a generation of its children. One of these indicators, supplied by the Children's Defense Fund, states that every three hours in this nation, a child is murdered.

Several comprehensive profiles of child victims have appeared over the last few years (Jenkins & Bell, 1992; Muscat, 1988; Silverman & Kennedy, 1993, pp. 179–188 [Canada]; Winpisinger, Hopkins, Indian, & Hostetler, 1991). Additionally, Katherine Christoffel's (1990) analyses of various U.S. nationwide data and Rosemary Gartner's (1991) aggregate analysis of the relationship between family structure and homicide victimization of children in 17 developed nations (including the U.S.), yield several risk factors for homicide against children.

When compared with child victims in general, more attention has been devoted to charting the social structures and processes associated with children who die specifically at the hands of parents. Chapter 7, "When Parents Kill Their Young Children: Detroit 1982–1986," examines such fatal incidents involving victims under the age of six years. It is of interest to observe that while parents who kill their young children are about evenly divided by gender, U.S. research focuses on homicidal mothers to the exclusion of homicidal fathers (Crimmins, Langley, Spunt, Brownstein, Cancel, Curry, Miller, & Sherman, 1993; Mann, 1993a; Weisheit, 1986). Additionally, I was able to locate one Canadian study of homicidal mothers (Silverman & Kennedy, 1993, pp. 155–158) and three non-U.S. Western studies of homicidal parents—defined collectively to include mothers and fathers (Silverman & Kennedy, 1993, pp. 77–81 [Canada]; Strang, 1993 [Australia]; Wilczynski & Morris, 1993 [England & Wales]).

Perhaps this attention on women offenders as mothers is a simple extension of the evident research fixation on homicidal women in general (see Introduction to Part II). Perhaps the outrageously "unnatural" act of a mother killing her own child requires more explanation than the less "unnatural" act of a father doing the same thing!

It should be noted that child victims of homicide represent a homicide type that is associated with low accountability. It is believed that populations and samples of child homicide victims based on coroner and criminal justice records "miss" or exclude more cases than most other types of homicide, a condition that may detract from the representativeness and generalizability of findings. Many childhood deaths resulting from abuse and neglect remain undetected (including infants killed and disposed of without their births being recorded) or are erroneously classified as accidents or sudden infant death syndrome (SIDS). Limited funds, training, time, or interest result in children being buried with their true cause of death hidden or overlooked. In the tiniest of victims, even competent investigators miss clues. For example, a baby can be shaken to death with no immediately apparent trace. This erroneous classification of death in children is concentrated in rural areas, where coroners are sometimes elected with little regard to training, competence, and credentials. Moreover, where neighborliness and familiarity are strong, as in small communities, investigators sometimes bypass child autopsies out of sympathy for a grieving family or because they believe the family members incapable of homicide (Allen, 1980, pp. 132–33; Viano, 1993, p. 98).

Child Victims of Homicide: A Portrait of Their Killers and the Circumstances of Their Deaths

6

Homicide is now one of the five leading causes of death among young children in this country (Thompson, Bernstein, & Connelly, 1980; Child Homicide—United States, 1982), and the United States ranks second among developed nations in childhood homicide rate (Christoffel & Liu, 1983). In spite of these figures, little research has focused on the subject (Adelson, 1961; Christoffel, 1988; Daly & Wilson, 1987; Fiala & Lafree, 1988; Totman, 1978, pp. 70–85; Weisheit, 1986). This study is designed to contribute to the development of a data base on children as homicide victims, in the interest of prevention through knowledge. The findings may also prove useful to scholars and practitioners in the development of programs, treatment modalities, and services designed for the particular needs of the survivors of such fatal dramas—the offenders and the families of both them and their victims.

RESEARCH METHODS

The subjects selected for this study include the total population of 93 arrestees accused of having killed persons under the age of 15 years in the city of Detroit, Michigan, between 1982 and 1986 (except those cases attributed to the negligent use of a

93

vehicle). A previously published study of parents accused of having killed their own children (Goetting, 1988d) drew from this data set. An important limitation of the study lies in its lack of generalizability. The study population includes a total of 93 offenders and 74 victims involved in 71 incidents, and represents 8.7% of all homicide arrestees in Detroit between 1982 and 1986. The data collection process took place in May of 1987 in the offices of the Homicide Section of the Detroit Police Department.

The data were tabulated and, when feasible, comparisons were made with the total population of Detroit arrestees for homicides committed during 1982 and 1983[1] and with previous homicide studies that did not control for age of victim. Since the proportion of homicide arrestees accused of having killed persons younger than 15 in this country hovers near 5%, this means that the comparisons employed should have utilized populations and samples constituting approximately 95% members accused of having killed persons older than 15 years. Clearly the comparisons applied in this study are less than ideal on two counts: (a) in terms of age of victim, the comparison criterion, the comparison groups are not totally mutually exclusive (i.e., the groups of offenders against adults contain some offenders against children) and (b) the comparison groups are not geographically and temporally comparable.

RESULTS

Demographic and Social Characteristics of Offenders and Victims

Race. Research has verified that homicide offenders and their victims are disproportionately Black. Detroit provides no exception to this generalization, and neither do the offenders against children in that city. In 1980, 63% of the Detroit population was Black (U.S. Bureau of the Census, 1983). Of all arrestees for homicides committed in Detroit during 1982 and 1983, 89.1% were Black, and 81.9% of victims were Black. Information on homicides against children indicates that a higher proportion of both killers and their victims (92.5% or 86 and 90.5% or 67, respectively) were Black.

Sex. Homicide offenders and victims are disproportionately male, and, again, Detroit data are consistent with that generalization. Approximately 82% of the 1982–83 general population of Detroit homicide arrestees and 77.2% of slain victims during those same years in that city were male. Among our population of offenders against children, 79.6% (74) were of that gender, as were 59.5% (44) of their victims. These data suggest that homicide against children, while still a predominantly masculine activity, may involve females to a greater extent than does homicide in general, especially where it relates to the victim.

Age. The study population of offenders varied widely in age between 13 and 70 years ($M = 25.5$; $SD = 9.7$). Their victims ranged in age from newborn to just days before the 15th birthday ($M = 7.3$; $SD = 5.7$). One-third of the victims were younger than two years.

Religious Affiliation of Offender. Of the 47 offenders for whom data were recorded, 34 (72.3%) were Protestant, 5 (10.6%) claimed a religious affiliation "other" than Protestant, Catholic or Jewish, and the remaining 8 (17%) claimed no religious affiliation.

Residential, Domestic, and Parental Status of Offender. All arrestees were residing in the Detroit area at the time of the offense. Most (91.4% or 74) of the 81 killers who reported residential status were living in a family setting; 2 (2.5%) resided with nonfamily, and the remaining 5 (6.2%) lived alone. Over 34% (28) of the 82 offenders for whom domestic status was recorded were living with a mate at the time of the fatal incident. Another half (41) were adults not living with mates. Thirteen (15.9%) were children, 12 of whom were living with their parent(s). Nearly 80% (53) of the 68 adult offenders were parents.

Residence and Family Background of Victim. All victims lived in Detroit at the time of the killing. Of the 61 children for whom information was available, 21 (34.4%) resided with their mothers and 1 (1.6%) with his father, in single-parent households. Another 10 (16.4%) lived with a parent and step-parent (or parent's lover) when the incident occurred. One child (1.6%) resided with each a grandmother, an aunt, a great aunt, and a mother's cousin. Two (3.3%) lived in foster homes, and another (1.6%) was a runaway from a state institution and living in a crack house selling crack. Two infants (3.3%) died at the hands of their mothers at birth, and therefore technically never had a domicile. Only 13 (21.3%) of these victims are known to have resided with both original parents when the offense took place. Another 7 (11.5%) lived with their mother, with the presence of the father or mother's mate unknown.

Social Class Indicators of Offender. Of the 62 offenders aged 18 and older for whom information on formal education was available, 36 (58.1%) had completed at least 12 years of school. Eight (13%) were educated beyond that level. These data reflect a somewhat depressed level of formal education when compared with the general population of United States adults at the same point in time.[2] Employment information was recorded for 73 of the arrestees who were 18 years of age and older at the time of the homicide. Over two-thirds of these offenders (68.5% or 50) were unemployed, two of whom were retired, and one of whom claimed disability compensation. These data on education and unemployment, in conjunction with the fact that 21 (27.3%) of the 77 subjects for whom information was available reported having no residential telephone,[3] are congruent with other studies, suggesting that homicide offenders are concentrated in the lower social classes (Bensing, Schroeder, & Jackson, 1960, p. 1289; Swigert & Farrell, 1978, p. 193; Wolfgang, 1958, pp. 36–39).

Arrest Record of Offender. Homicide records indicate that at least 61.2% of the 85 offenders who were aged 15 or older had been arrested at least once prior to the offenses that predisposed them into the study population. While this is a crude measure of criminal history, since it fails to delineate the particular charges and dispositions associated with arrests, it does suggest that a high proportion of the killers under observation here are likely to have had criminal backgrounds. This 61.2% is in line with general populations of homicide offenders on this dimension. Wolfgang (1958, p. 175) reports 64% and Swigert and Farrell (1978, p. 194) report 56% of their homicide offender populations as having had previous arrests.

Demographic, Social, and Residential Relationships Between Offenders and Victims

Prior Social Relationship and Residential Relationship. Most reported killings in this country occur between persons who have had some prior relationship. Between 1980 and 1985 only 13.3% to 17.6% of homicides involved persons unknown to one another. In Detroit during the years 1982 and 1983, 19.1% of the 628 homicidal relationships[4] for which information has been recorded were categorized as "stranger." Among the present study population the proportion is larger. Nearly one-third (30 or 31.3%) of these 96 relationships was that of stranger. Just over one-quarter (25 or 26%) was parent–child (one adoptive) and another 13 (13.5%) involved the parent's spouse or boyfriend/ girlfriend. One (1%) involved an aunt, 1 (1%) a cousin, 2 (2.1%) a foster parent, and 1 (1%) a mother's cousin. Nearly 16 (17%) were characterized by acquaintanceship, and 7 (7.3%) by friend- ship. It is interesting to note that none of these homicides oc- curred between siblings.

For 37.5% of these relationships, the offender and victim shared residence at the time of the offense.

Demographic Relationships: Race, Sex, and Age. Homicide offenders and their victims are nearly always of the same race (Bensing et al., 1960, p. 51; Block, 1976, p. 498; Swigert & Farrell, 1978, p. 197; Voss & Hepburn, 1968, p. 59). In Detroit during 1982

and 1983, 91.4% of the 669 homicidal relationships for which
information is available were intraracial: 82.7% were Black-on-
Black, and the remaining 8.7% were White-on-White. The present
study indicates a similar proportion, 90.7% (87), of intraracial
killing: 86.5% (83) of those cases were Black-on-Black, and the
remaining 4.2% (4) were White-on-White. In those instances
where members of the offender population killed across racial
lines (9.4% or 9), twice as many Blacks killed Whites as vice versa
(6.3% or 6 compared with 3.1% or 3). That fact is basically congruent with information describing the 1982–83 general population of Detroit homicides and with findings of the other homicide
studies cited above, all of which demonstrate a higher proportion of Blacks killing Whites. The 1982–83 general homicide data
show that 6.4% of those deadly relationships were Black-on-
White, and 2.1% were White-on-Black.

Homicide generally occurs between members of the same sex,
and most of such intrasexual incidents involve males. Relatively
few females kill, but when they do, their victims are almost always
males (Bensing et al., 1960, p. 57; Block, 1976, p. 498; Gibbons,
1973, p. 361; Swigert & Farrell, 1978, p. 197; Voss & Hepburn,
1968, p. 503; Wilbanks, 1983b, p. 10, 1983a, p. 304). In Detroit
during 1982 and 1983, 66.4% of the 669 homicidal relationships
for which information is available were intrasexual; 63.8% involved males, and the remaining 2.5% involved females. The research population of offenders against children demonstrates a
slightly lower proportion of intrasexual homicidal relationships:
59.4% (57) in total, with 13 cases (13.5%) involving females.
Nearly 41% (40) of the relationships crossed gender lines, 32.3%
(31) being male-on-female, and the remaining 8.5% (8) being
female-on-male. These two proportions deviate quite distinctly
from the 15.7% and 17.9%, respectively, associated with the
1982–83 Detroit general homicide populations. Most of the differences observed between the general Detroit data and our study
population data on this point of victim–offender gender relationship are a reflection of the disproportionately high component
of females associated with this study population, especially as
victims.

All except 2 (97.9% or 94) of the homicidal relationships under observation here involved a victim younger than his/her slayer. In the cases of these two exceptions, the victim and offender were the same age. This situation deviates greatly from that associated with the 1982–83 general Detroit homicide population, where 47.5% of the victims were younger: 45.2% were older, and the remaining 7.3% were the same age. Furthermore, the mean difference in age between these offenders and their young victims was larger than that associated with the general population—18.5 years compared with 12.8 years. These data suggest that offenders against children differ from the general population of homicide offenders in degree but not in direction of age difference between them and their victims. They appear to select victims who deviate more from themselves in age, with that difference (consistent with that of the general population of offenders) in the direction of being younger.

Circumstances of Offense

General Social Context. The killings observed among this population of offenders against children occurred in a variety of contexts. While most (67.6% or 50) of the 74 homicides were interpersonal acts of passion, nearly one-fourth (18) were the result of accident (as determined by the researcher) or mental incompetence, and 8.1% (6) were committed in the context of another crime. The 74 victims met their deaths under the following circumstances:

  1 male child,

16 female infants, and

11 male infants were beaten (21), shaken (3), scalded (2), suffocated (1) or dropped off of a bridge (1) by parents and/or other caretakers;

  2 male children (along with their mother) were shot by a man who was father to one and stepfather to the other;

  1 female infant was administered an insulin shot by her mother to prevent a scheduled loss of custody;

1 female infant was accidentally left to suffocate in a plastic sheet by her foster mother;

2 female infants and

2 male infants died of neglect at the hands of their mentally incompetent mothers;

7 male children and

2 female children were shot (all by males) in the context of gun play;

6 male children were shot (5) or stabbed (1) (all by males) in retaliation against the victim;

2 female adolescents were shot (both by males) in retaliation against the victim in drug-related incidents;

5 male children were shot (3) or burned to death (2) (all by males) in the context of retaliation against a relative or friend of the victim;

4 victims were shot (3) or raped, strangled and burned to death (1) (all by males) while being victimized of robbery (3) or burglary (1);

2 male adolescents were shot (both by males) in their acts of burglary;

3 victims received bullets intended for someone else (two perpetrators were male, one female);

3 male adolescents were killed (by other male adolescents) in the context of a quarrel;

1 female child was sexually assaulted and strangled (by a male stranger); and

3 males (aged 8, 12 and 13) received stray bullets in incidents totally unrelated to them (all perpetrators were male).

Homicidal Method. Firearms are the most common means of inflicting death in the United States. Between 1968 and 1978 the proportion of homicides committed with firearms varied between 63% and 65.7% (Riedel, Zahn, & Mock, 1985, p. 48). In Detroit during 1982–83, 65.8% of the 1,138 reported homicides were shootings. Another 17.8% were stabbings, 11.4% were beatings, 0.7% were burnings, and 4.2% were conducted by some other means. The distribution of homicidal methods associated with this population of young victims differs from that associated with the 1982–83 general population of victims primarily in that a considerably lower proportion of the children (43.2% or 32) died of gunshot wounds, and a considerably higher proportion (33.8% or 25) were beaten to death, 15 (20.3%) with blunt instruments, and 10 (13.5%) through use of hands and/or feet as weapons. Another 6.8% (5) were burned to death. Three (4.1%) each were stabbed, strangled, or suffocated. One victim (1.4%) each was drowned and poisoned, and 4 (5.4%) were allowed to die of neglect.

Number of Victims and Offenders. Almost all homicides are one-on-one incidents. Detroit provides no exception to this generalization, and neither do the offenses in that city involving children as victims. In Detroit during 1982 and 1983, 87.9% of the 578 homicidal incidents for which information is available involved a single victim and a single offender. Another 10.6% of those offenses were single-victim/multiple-offender; 1.4% were multiple-victim/single-offender and the remaining 0.2% were multiple-victim/multiple-offender offenses. This research population of 71 homicidal incidents involving children as victims demonstrated a somewhat lower proportion of single-victim offenses, and accordingly a somewhat higher proportion of multiple-victim offenses. Approximately 76% (54) of these killings were one-on-one. Another 12.7% (9) involved a single victim and multiple offenders, including 6 cases of 2 offenders, 2 cases of 3 offenders, and 1 case of 8 offenders. Nearly 9% (6) of the deadly events were multiple-victim/single-offender in nature, 5 involving 2 victims and 1 involving 3 victims. Finally, 2 homicides (2.8%) involved multiple victims and offenders.

Spatial Considerations. Offenders against children are more likely to kill in the private residence setting than are other offenders. Over three-quarters (75.7% or 56) of the deaths under observation here took place in a home: 14.9% (11) occurred at the residence of the victim, 10.8% (8) at the residence of the offender, 43.2% (32) at the residence of both, and 6.8% (5) at another residence. Additionally, 18.9% (14) of the killings took place on public streets, and 1.4% (1) each in a school, a store, a "dope house," and the basement of the apartment structure shared by the victim and offender.

Approximately 9% (4) of the 43 Detroit offenses committed at a private residence for which information was available occurred outside the actual residence, usually on the porch or in the yard. Nearly 42% (18) occurred in a bedroom, 30.1% (13) in the living room, 9.3% (4) in the kitchen, and 2.3% (1) in each the basement, the dining room, a hallway, and a closet.

Temporal Considerations. For 1982 and 1983 combined, the frequency distribution of Detroit homicides over the 12 months indicates a general overall stability except for slight increases during August–September (the hot season) and December–January (the holiday season), and a discernable dip in April (the introduction to spring). Child victims, however, displayed no apparent seasonal fluctuations. Their frequencies over the 12 months appear to be randomly distributed, with a high of 12.3% in March, September, and December, and a low of 5.5% in February, April, and July.

Relative to days of week and hours of day, the research population demonstrated virtually no conformity to the norm. Data are consistent in indicating that homicide is concentrated during weekends, but the offenses against children observed here provide an exception to that generalization. While studies of general homicide populations suggest that between 56.6% and 84% of deadly encounters occur on Fridays, Saturdays, and Sundays (the days with the three highest single frequencies), only one-third (23) of this population of 69 children for which information is known met their deaths on those three days. Compared with homicides perpetrated by general populations, those under consideration here are distributed more evenly throughout the week, with Monday, Tuesday, and Wednesday tying at the highest frequency (17.4% or 12), and Saturday the lowest (7.2% or 5).

Wolfgang (1958) and Pokorney (1965) provide the only two sources of information on homicide that effectively can be compared with data describing these Detroit offenders against children on the subject of time of offense.[5] The two studies are consistent with one another in indicating that approximately half of homicides occur between 8:00 P.M. and 1:59 A.M., and another quarter occur between 2:00 P.M. and 7:59 P.M. Far fewer than half (34.8% or 23) of the 66 child victims for whom information was available died between 8:00 P.M. and 1:59 A.M., and nearly as many, 31.8% or 21, were killed between 2:00 P.M. and 7:59 P.M. Another 22.7% (15) were killed between 8:00 A.M. and 1:59 P.M., and the remaining 10.6% (7) died between 2:00 A.M. and 7:59 P.M.

Audience and Offender's Response. Nearly 60% (41) of the 69 victims for whom data were recorded were killed before witnesses. Most (52.5% or 47) of the 90 offenders for whom information was available remained at the homicide scene or with the victim at the hospital until authorities arrived. One offender (1.1%) committed suicide at the scene.

Arrest Disposition

Prosecuting Attorney. Of the 79 offenders for whom information was available who were at risk of prosecution (excluding the 12 who were processed by the juvenile court, and the 1 suicide), 16.5% (13) were denied a warrant for criminal charge by the prosecutor. This proportion suggests a strong bias against this population of offenders in light of the fact that an estimated 30.4% of the general population of homicide arrestees for that city during 1983 enjoyed similar denial.[6] Further analyses controlling for severity of offense and other factors are necessary in order to properly question prosecutorial bias as it may apply to homicide offenders against children.

Court. Three of the 66 arrested adults for whom data were recorded who were processed by the court (5.5%) had charges dismissed by the judge at the preliminary hearing. Over 65% (43)

were convicted of murder or manslaughter; 1.5% (1) were convicted of another felony; 7.6% (5) were convicted of a misdemeanor; 18.2% (12) were acquitted; and 2.2% (2) were found not
guilty by reason of insanity. Of the 49 convicted arrestees, 43
(87.7%) received prison sentences: 9 for life, and the rest for a
mean minimum of 15 years. A total of 40 of the 43 offenders
convicted of murder or manslaughter (93%) were sentenced to
incarceration. Three other misdemeanor convicts received prison
sentences.

DISCUSSION

The construction of a statistical profile describing the population of all 93 persons arrested for killing persons under the age
of 15 years in the predominantly Black city of Detroit, Michigan,
between 1982 and 1986, yields the image of a locally born Black
Detroit man in his middle 20s who is a Protestant, unmarried
(legally or by common-law) parent living in a family setting. He
is undereducated, unemployed, and has an arrest record. His
relationship with a male child who is a family member or friend,
and also Black, is severed by a gunshot or beating in a bedroom
or living room of a private residence between 2:00 P.M. and
1:59 A.M.

It appears from this Detroit study that while offenses against
children are subject in general to homicide patterns characteristic of other interpersonal killings, they perhaps deviate somewhat
from those norms along certain dimensions. Such offenses may
more likely involve females, especially as victims, and the offenders may select victims who are more different from themselves
in age, with that difference being in the direction of being
younger. A higher proportion of these brutal acts may victimize
strangers, may be inflicted through beatings, and may occur in
a private residence. They may be more evenly distributed over
the months of the year, days of the week, and hours of the day.

If this research dispels any myths about the typical child victim of homicide, it is perhaps the myth that there is a typical

victim. The child victim of homicide is not usually the adolescent killed in gang activity or the unwanted infant killed by a parent. The grisly descriptions of varied victim–offender relationships and circumstances of offense are chilling precisely because there is no common denominator other than indifference to life (Robbins, 1990).

It is interesting to note that early in 1987, a local support group known as SOSAD, for Save Our Sons and Daughters, "dedicated to keeping alive the memory of young people killed in Detroit's continuing orgy of violence," emerged to protest youth-on-youth violence, and to prod the city and state into dealing more forcefully with the problem ("Saving the Children," 1988; "SOSAD: Detroiters Will No Longer Stand," 1987). The organization, which includes some parents of slain youngsters, has sponsored public prayer events, and supports a range of care for troubled youth—from more motivational and educational programs for the very young and emotionally disturbed to more detention facilities for the very dangerous and disruptive. About a third (25) of the victims associated with this study qualify as referents for SOSAD.

NOTES

1. These data were selected for comparison because of their availability. They had been computed by this author for a previous study (Goetting, 1988a).

2. The proportion of noninstitutionalized Americans aged 25 and older who had completed four years of high school increased progressively from an estimated 70.9% in 1982 to an estimated 74.7% in 1986 (U.S. Bureau of the Census, 1982–86).

3. This proportion is high when compared with the estimated 10.4% of Detroit residences reportedly having no telephone service in January of 1986 (Cross, 1986).

4. Throughout this section, entitled Demographic and Social Relationships Between Offenders and Victims, the data describing homicidal relationships characteristic of the general 1982–83 Detroit homicide population take into consideration all relationships associated with not only single-offender/single-victim killings, but also with multiple-

offender or multiple-victim offenses or both. This means that the number of homicidal relationships associated with a certain analysis is greater than the number of actual homicides involved. The research population data on offenders against children with which these general data are compared include information on 93 offenders and 73 victims involved in 96 victim–offender relationships, including 6 double-offender/single-child victim, 1 quadruple-offender/single-child victim, 18-offender/single-child victim, and 3 single offender/double-child victim incidents. Only child victims are included in the analyses. The 8 adult co-victims in 5 of the homicidal incidents are excluded from these comparative analyses of demographic and social homicidal relationships.

5. Only those two studies utilized a coding scheme for hour of offense similar to that employed for the present study.

6. The computation of this estimate can be found in an earlier Detroit homicide study conducted by Goetting (1988a).

When Parents Kill Their Young Children: Detroit 1982–1986

7

INTRODUCTION

Brenda was a 22-year-old unmarried Black mother of four pre-school children. She had an 11th grade education and was employed at a local discount store. Her youngest son, Bryon, now 2½ years of age, had been born prematurely, weighing 3 lb. and with a malfunctioning brain. Brenda had an active file with Protective Services, who petitioned, without success, to have Bryon removed from her custody the year before due to failure to provide proper medical attention. At dinnertime one Thursday in November, Bryon refused his food. Brenda placed him in the bathtub and turned on the hot water. After he had been scalded to death, she laid him out on the dining room floor, telling the other children to kiss him because he was dead. Brenda was found guilty of Involuntary Manslaughter, and sentenced to serve 4½ to 15 years in prison.

Patricia was a 20-year-old Black and unemployed welfare recipient. She was separated from her husband who was the father of her only child, 16-month-old Craig. Patricia's boyfriend was Kevin, a 23-year-old unmarried and unemployed Black man with no children and a high school education. One Friday evening in February, Patricia and Kevin met at the home of some friends to spend the weekend together. Patricia brought Craig, and the three of them stayed together in the attic bedroom. Late Sunday night everyone in the household was preparing to retire. Patricia, Craig, and Kevin were in their room watching television, and the baby was nearly asleep. Patricia went downstairs to wash out some things, to prepare a bowl of cereal for a friend, and to use the bathroom. When she returned, the child was crying and Kevin was in the process of hanging up his belt. Patricia told Kevin that he had no right to hit her baby. He retorted that he had hit Craig because the child had urinated on himself. Then he hit Patricia in the face and left the room in anger. Craig died at the hospital 2 hr later of injuries from the beating. Kevin had spanked the child on previous occasions, as well as having threatened Patricia's life at least once. Two friends and Kevin drove Patricia from the hospital to one of their homes where she could rest. On that trip Kevin did not mention the dead child, but attempted to convince Patricia that he loved her and was going to take good care of her. Kevin was charged with second degree murder, but was acquitted by a jury.

These cases describe 2 of the 33 incidents involving parents or parent figures who are reported to have killed their child or charge who was under the age of 6 years in Detroit, Michigan, between 1982 and 1986. Since the discovery of "the battered child syndrome" in 1962 (Kempe, Silverman, Steele, Droegemveller, & Silver, 1962), much research attention has been devoted to child abuse in the United States. However, very little of this effort (Myers, 1970; Resnick, 1969, 1970; Scott, 1973; Totman, 1978; Weisheit, 1986) has focused on the most extreme form of parental violence against children: filicide, or the killing of a child by his parent. This study is designed to contribute to the development of a data base on children as victims of parental violence, particularly filicide, in the interest of prevention through increased knowledge. The findings may also prove useful to researchers and practitioners in the development of programs, treatment modalities, and services designed for the particular needs of the survivors of such fatal acts. It is the intention of this research to explore the types of people who kill their small children and the circumstances surrounding such events.

The subjects selected for this investigation include the total population of 36 parents or parent figures arrested for killing their children or charges who were under the age of 6 years (except those attributed to the negligent use of a vehicle) in the city of Detroit, Michigan, between 1982 and 1986, and their 34 victims. Twenty-one (56.8%) of the arrestees were natural parents, 11 (27.7%) were step-parents or boyfriends/girlfriends of the natural parents, 2 (5.4%) were foster parents, and 1 (2.7%) each was an adoptive parent, an aunt with legal custody, and a mother's cousin with legal custody. An important limitation of this study lies in its lack of generalizability. Data collection was carried out in May 1987 in the offices of the Homicide section of the Detroit Police Department. Police-recorded information regarding each case, including the Investigator's Report, Interrogation Record, and Witness Statement was electronically copied for subsequent perusal.

THE OFFENDERS

The offenders were about evenly divided by gender: 52.8% (19) were female, and 47.2% (17) were male. They ranged in age from 16 to 39 years, with a mean of 26.4 and a standard deviation of 5.9 years of age. Thirty-three (91.7%) were Black, and the remaining three (8.3%) were White. Sixteen of the 19 subjects for whom data were recorded (84.2%) were Protestant. All subjects were residents of Detroit. Of the 30 for whom information was reported, 24 (76.7%) had originated in the North Central portion of the United States (applying the geographic grouping of states adopted by the U.S. Bureau of Census), all but five of them in Detroit. The remaining 23.3% (7) were Southern born. Over half (55.9% or 19) of the 34 offenders for whom information was available were living with a mate at the time of the killing. Sixty-nine percent (20) of the 29 subjects for whom data were recorded had achieved at least a high school education,[1] 16.7% (6) had completed additional formal schooling. Over two-thirds (23) of the 32 subjects for whom data were available were unemployed at the time of the killing, one claiming disability compensation; and at least one-fourth (9) of the total population of offenders were recipients of welfare. Again, this information on education, unemployment, and welfare status, in conjunction with the fact that 36.4% (12) of the 33 subjects for whom data were available reported having no residential telephone,[2] is congruent with other studies suggesting that homicide offenders are concentrated in the lower social classes (Bensing et al., 1960, pp. 128–129; Swigert & Farrell, 1978, p. 193; Wolfgang, 1958, pp. 36–39). Information on previous arrests indicated that 14 of the 24 offenders for whom data were available (58.%) had been arrested prior to the incident under observation here.

THE VICTIMS AND CIRCUMSTANCES

The 34 young children were killed in the 33 incidents under the following circumstances:

6 girls were beaten by their mothers; in two cases the mother's husband was a co-offender

1 girl was administered an insulin shot by her mother to prevent a scheduled loss of custody

1 girl was smothered by her mother

2 girls and

2 boys died of neglect at the hands of their mentally-incompetent mothers

1 boy was scalded in bathwater by his mother (Bryon)

1 boy received a bullet from his mother intended for his father

1 girl was left accidentally to suffocate in a plastic sheet by her foster mother

1 boy was beaten by his foster mother

3 girls and

2 boys were beaten by their fathers; in one case the father's common-law wife was a co-offender

1 girl and

1 boy were shaken to death by their fathers

1 boy was dropped off a bridge in a premeditated fashion by his father

3 girls and

3 boys were beaten by their mothers' husbands or boyfriends (Craig)

1 girl was scalded in bathwater by her mother's common-law husband

1 girl was beaten by her father's common-law wife

1 boy was shaken and

1 boy was beaten by legal guardians; in the former case the guardian was the mother's older sister, and in the latter case she was the mother's cousin.

Approximately 59% (20) of the victims were male. They ranged in age from newborn to 5½ years ($\bar{X}$ = 1.6, SD = 1.3 years of age). Over 94% (32) were Black. As expected, all 37 homicidal relationships were intraracial. Again as expected, all victims, like their assailants, were Detroit residents. For nearly all of the homicidal relationships (86.5% or 32), the child lived with the killer at the time of the fatal incident.

Most homicides are single-victim/single-offender incidents, and this population of parents and parental figures provides no exception to that generalization. Only 27% (7) of these offenders were participants in something other than a one-on-one incident. One perpetrated a double killing: a set of infant twin daughters were allowed to starve by their mother. The remaining six offenders consisted of three parents (two mothers and a father) who, in cooperation with their spouses, beat their daughters to death.

All except one of the killings under scrutiny here were executed in a private residence; the exception involved the boy who was dropped off of a bridge by his father. Twelve of the 31 offenders for whom information was available (38.7%) displayed their destructive behavior in view of at least one bystander. In all cases, these observers were family members, usually siblings of the victims. This proportion is lower than the 54.4% found in the Swigert and Farrell (1978) homicide study (Felson & Steadman, 1983, p. 73).

Although homicide is known to vary systematically by month of year (Goetting, 1992), day of week, and hour of day, no such patterns are discernable from this small population of filicides. Perhaps filicide is not subject to the leisure-related temporal order of homicide in general. Instead, it may be subject to more subtle dynamics inherent in the parent–child relationship.

Most parents under observation remained at the homicide scene or with the victim until investigators arrived; only 5.7% (2) fled to avoid detection.

ARREST AND COURT DISPOSITIONS

Eleven percent (4) of the offenders in this study were denied warrant by the Prosecuting Attorney. This is discernably low when compared with the estimated 30.4% of the general population of Detroit homicide arrestees during 1983 who were similarly denied warrant.[3] Perhaps judgments are harsher on homicidal parents because their victims are viewed as defenseless, and because killing one's child is so totally antithetic to the parental role. Further analyses controlling for severity of crime and other factors are necessary to properly pursue the question of prosecutoral bias applied to this category of homicide offenders.

Two of the 31 (6.5%) arrestees who were processed by the Court as adults (this is excluding the 16-year-old mother accused of having beaten her infant daughter, who was processed by the Juvenile Court) had charges dismissed by the judge at the preliminary hearing. Over 67% (21) were convicted of Murder or Manslaughter and one subject was convicted of Cruelty to a Child, another felony. Approximately 16% (5) were acquitted, and the remaining 6.5% (2) were found Not Guilty by Reason of Insanity. Of the 22 convicted arrestees, 81.8% (18) received prison sentences: one for life, and the rest showing a minimum sentence with a mean of 13.4 and a standard deviation of 17.2 years.

DISCUSSION

The construction of a statistical profile describing the population 36 parents or parent figures arrested for killing their children or charges who were under the age of 6 years in Detroit, Michigan, between 1982 and 1986 yields the image of a locally born, Protestant, Black man or woman in his or her middle 20s, who is married and residing with the family. He or she is undereducated, unemployed, and has an arrest record. The parent–child relationship is severed in a rage of impatience and anger at a private residence as a result of beating or shaking.

What emerges through careful inspection of the police documents describing this small population of filicides is the portrayal of a young nontraditional minority family disadvantaged along multiple dimensions, and in many ways isolated from mainstream culture. The parents, for the most part, are living in loosely structured marital relationships, and are poorly equipped to overcome the daily mundane struggles imposed on them by their oppressed worlds of racism, sexism, poverty, mental illness, and general social disorganization. They are drastically limited in the educational and occupational resources and in the social skills required to maintain a life of comfort and dignity in the United States today. As mentioned elsewhere, their knowledge of the street scene is particularly keen, yet they are shrouded in ignorance in other areas critical to their sense of well-being, such as their ability to parent effectively. The example, also cited earlier, of such ignorance was a precipitating factor in one of the deadly incidents included in this study. A woman beat her young daughter to death and argued convincingly that the child had *refused* to mind by continuing to dirty her pants in spite of constant reprimands. Such behavior on the part of the child was attributed by the mother to a willful lack of compliance, and to stubbornness deserving of punitive sanction. This woman failed to understand that in the early years of life, a child's psychomuscular constitution may not yet be fully developed to control eliminative functions. Having that knowledge may have eased the burden of parenthood significantly for this woman, providing a source of tolerance necessary to the vitality of the parent–child relationship.

Alleviation of the type of violence and neglect outlined in this chapter would require preventive consideration beyond those of a reformative nature. While piecemeal efforts to counter the conditions that breed this kind of behavior may furnish temporary mitigation to some, they may in the long run perpetuate those conditions by providing a false sense of relief and equity.

NOTES

1. This proportion is slightly low when compared with those representing noninstitutionalized Americans aged 25 and older who had completed four years of high school. Those figures progressed from an estimated 70.9% in 1982 to an estimated 74.7% in 1986 (U.S. Bureau of Census, 1982–86). If age were controlled in the comparison between these research subjects and the general population of the United States, the research subjects would be undereducated to a much greater extent.

2. This proportion is high when compared with the estimated 10.4% of Detroit residences reportedly having no telephone service in January of 1986 (Cross, 1986).

3. This estimate was computed by dividing the number of warrants issued by the Office of Wayne County Prosecuting Attorney in 1983 for Murder and Manslaughter in the city of Detroit (296) (Smith, 1985) by the total number of 1983 arrests for Murder and Manslaughter recorded by the Homicide Section of the Detroit Department of Police (425); by their transforming that quotient (0.696) to a percentage by multiplying by 100 (69.6%), this represents the proportion of arrestees who were issued warrants; and by subtracting that percentage from 100 (30.4%).

Homicidal Children

V

Introduction to Part V

Juvenile violence has emerged as an issue of critical concern to the well-being of our nation. Along with the high rate of murdered children as an indicator of national child neglect is the correspondingly high rate of homicides perpetrated by children. Most youth are killed by other youth (Jenkins & Bell, 1992, p. 72). National Center for Juvenile Justice data inform us that in the last five years the number of murders committed by youths under the age of 18 has skyrocketed by 85% (Ingrassia, Annin, Biddle, & Miller, 1993, p. 17). Chapter 8, "Patterns of Homicide Among Children," provides a comprehensive profile of homicides perpetrated by children under the age of 15 years.

While most research on homicidal children comes from small clinical populations and samples, some important epidemiologic information has been produced. It should be noted that in most, if not all, of that work, the age criterion for subjects is under 18 years rather than under 15, as employed in Chapter 8. That age difference may affect research results. Homicide committed by preadolescent children may be qualitatively different than that committed by adolescents. Dewey Cornell (1989, p. 23) suggests that young children have a limited understanding of death and that, as a result, their aggressive behavior may be more impulsive and less goal directed than in adolescence.

While comprehensive profiles on homicidal children continue to surface (Rowley, Ewing, & Singer, 1987; Cornell, Benedek, & Benedek, 1987; Cheatwood & Block, 1990; Jenkins & Bell, 1992; Silverman & Kennedy, 1993, pp. 158–166 [Canada]; Ewing, 1990), recent work tends to focus on subgroups. Gang homicide (Maxson, Gordon, & Klein, 1985; Curry & Spergel, 1988; Huff, 1990; Covey, Menard, & Franzese, 1992; Block & Block, 1993; Conly, Kelly, Mahanna, & Warner, 1993) as well as parricide (Mones, 1991; Heide 1993a, 1993b, 1994a, 1994b; Crimmins, 1993) have been vigorously explored.

Patterns of Homicide Among Children

8

Very little sociological information is available regarding homicidal children. Four such inquiries have been conducted (Hamparian, Davis, Jacobson, & McGraw, 1985; Hamparian, Schuster, Dinitz, & Conrad, 1978; Strasburg, 1978; Zimring, 1984); other material on the subject has been psychological and psychoanalytical in nature, reflecting observations of small, opportunity, and usually clinical samples (Adelson, 1973; Anthony & Rizzo, 1973; Gardiner, 1976; Godwin, 1978, Ch. 4; Heide, 1986; Leborici, 1973; Lewis et al., 1985; Lewis, Shanok, Grant, & Ritvo, 1983; Mack, Scherl, & Macht, 1973; Russell, 1979; Sorrells, 1977, 1980). This study describes the circumstances surrounding homicides perpetrated by children. The purpose of this chapter is to contribute to the development of an empirical data base on violent, and in particular, homicidal, youth in the interest of prevention through knowledge.

METHODS

The subjects selected for this study include all arrestees[1] for homicide (except those attributed to the negligent use of a vehicle) committed in the city of Detroit, Michigan, between 1977 and 1984 who were under the age of 15 years at the time of the offense. The study population includes a total of 55 offenders associated with the slaying of 48 victims. These 55 offenders represent approximately 1.8% of all homicide arrestees in that city during those eight years. Data collection took place in June of 1985 in the offices of the Homicide Section of the Detroit Police Department and the Deputy Chief of the Wayne County Juvenile Court. Police- and Court-recorded information regarding each case, including the Investigator's Report, Interrogation Record, Witness Statements, and Case Histories was electronically copied for subsequent perusal.

The data were tabulated and, when feasible, comparisons are made with the total population of Detroit arrestees for homicides committed during 1982 and 1983,[2] and with previous homicide studies that did not control for age of offender, and therefore based their findings nearly totally on cases involving offenders aged 15 and older. Since the proportion of homicide arrestees who are younger than 15 consistently hovers near 1%, this means that the comparison studies utilized populations and samples constituting approximately 99% members who were 15 years of age and older. Clearly the comparisons applied for this study are less than ideal on two counts: (1) in terms of offender age, the comparison criterion, comparison groups are not totally mutually exclusive (i.e., the nonjuvenile group contains some juvenile members) and (2) except when 1982 and 1983 Detroit data are available, the comparison groups are not geographically and temporally comparable.

RESULTS

The information reported herein is presented through use of the four-part organizational scheme employed throughout this book.

Demographic and Social Characteristics of Offenders and Victims

Race. Research repeatedly has verified that homicide offenders and their victims are disproportionately Black. Detroit provides no exception to this generalization, and neither do the child killers in that city. In 1980 (the year for which the most recent data are available), 63% of the Detroit population were Black (U.S. Bureau of the Census, 1983). Of all arrestees for homicides committed in Detroit during 1982 and 1983, 89.1% were Black, and 81.9% of victims were Black. Information on our young population indicates that while about the same proportion of offenders were Black (85.5% or 47), a lower proportion of their victims (68.8% or 33) were of that racial category. These data suggest that while child killers are racially similar to their older counterparts, they are less likely to select Blacks as their victims.

Sex. Homicide offenders and victims are disproportionately male, and, again, Detroit data are consistent with that generalization. Approximately 82% of the 1982–1983 age-general population of Detroit homicide arrestees and 77.2% of slain victims during those same years in that city were male. Among our population of child offenders, 98.2% (54) were of that gender, as were 83.3% (40) of their victims. These Detroit data suggest that homicides perpetrated by children may involve males to a greater extent than do other homicides.

Race and Sex Combined. Considering race and sex simultaneously, it becomes apparent that Black males in this young Detroit population made up 81.8% (45) of all homicide arrestees. White males and Black females followed distantly with 12.7% (7) and 1.8% (1), respectively. This frequency distribution is somewhat inconsonant with that describing the age-general population of arrested killers in Detroit during 1982 and 1983. Black males made up 73.8% of those offenders, followed by Black females, White males, and White females, constituting 14.9%, 9.6%, and 1.4% of that total distribution, respectively. The combined race and sex distribution of the slain victims of the study population, when compared with that of their counterpart age-general population, reflects a somewhat lower proportion of Black males and Black females, and accordingly, a higher proportion of White males and White females. Of the victims of the child killers, Black males made up 60.4% (29), followed by White males, Black females, and White females at 20.8% (10), 8.3% (4), and 6.3% (3), respectively. Of the victims of the age-general population of arrestees, Black males made up 66.5%, while Black females, White males, and White females constituted 15.4%, 13.6%, and 4.2%, respectively.

Age. The study population of offenders ranged in age between 3 and 14 years, having a mean of 12.7 years and a standard deviation of 2.1 years. Their victims varied widely in age from one to 94 years, with a mean of 27.7 years and a standard deviation of 24.8 years. Four of the victims were infants aged 3 or younger, and another six were 65 or older.

Birthplace and Residence. All arrestees and their victims were residing in the city of Detroit at the time of the offense. The great majority (82.9% or 29) of the 35 killers for whom information was available were born in Michigan, and most (93.1% or 27) of those in Detroit. Two others were from Ohio and Missouri; and the remaining 4 were Southern born.[3]

Of the 50 arrestees for whom information was available, 44% (22) resided with their mothers and 4% (2) with their fathers in single-parent households. Another 8% (4) lived with a parent and stepparent when the incident occurred. In total, 12% (6) resided with no parents or stepparents but with other relatives, all but one of those being with grandparents. Three (6%) children lived with a parent and the parent's lover, and another one (2%) lived with his own lover. One (2%) offender was committed to a child care institution, but had run away and for fifteen days had been living with friends. Only 22% (11) of these young killers resided with both original parents when the offense took place, which generally is consistent with findings from other studies of violent youth (Fagan, Piper, & Moore, 1985, Appendix B; Hartsone & Hansen, 1984, p. 93; MacNamara & Sagarin, 1986, p. 313; Solway, Richardson, Hays, & Elion, 1981, p. 201).

The history of the residential guardianship status of this study population of homicidal children reflects instability. Nearly two-thirds (64.5% or 20) of the 31 subjects for whom information was recorded had changed residential guardianship at least once in their lives. Seven (22.6%) had undergone one such change, 6 (19.4%) had experienced two, 2 (6.5%) had experienced three, and 5 (16.1%) had changed four or more times. Typically these changes involved a parental separation, some of which were followed by a remarriage and/or a transfer of custody to a relative, usually grandparent(s).

Information on type of residential structure was available for 35 of the 55 offenders. Nearly two-thirds (65.7% or 23) of them lived in single-family dwellings, at least eight of which were being purchased by their families. Ten (28.6%) resided in apartment complexes, and the remaining two (5.8%) lived in duplexes.

None of the 30 killers for whom data were available lived alone. The number of persons constituting the residential unit varied between two and eight, with a mean of 4.7 persons and a standard deviation of 1.6 persons.

Previous Police Contact of Offender. For most (59.4% or 19) of the 32 subjects for whom data were available, the homicide that predisposed them to this study population was a first offense. The remaining 40.6% (13) reportedly had experienced at least one prior police contact. It is interesting to note that about the same proportion (36% or 9) of the 25 for whom information was recorded were described by guardians and/or teachers as discipline problems.

The Families of Offenders

The original parents of only 11 (29.7%) of the 37 homicidal children for whom information was available were married and living together at the time of the offense. Three (8.1%) marriages had been terminated by the death of the husband. Fifteen (40.5%) sets of parents had separated or divorced. The remaining 8 (21.6%) had never married. At least 5 sets of natural parents evidently married after the birth of the subject, since our data show that 13 (39.4% of the 33 offenders for whom information was recorded) subjects were born illegitimately.

Consider the current domestic status of those parents who were no longer together when the homicide occurred. Of the 23 living mothers for whom data were available, 17 (73.9%) had no current mate. Three (13%) were remarried and living with a husband, and another 3 (13%) were participants in a common-law marriage. A much higher proportion of the fathers were currently remarried. Of the 12 living fathers for whom information was available, 7 (58.3%) were currently remarried and residing with wife. Another 2 (16.7%) were involved in a common-law marriage. Only one-fourth (3) of these fathers had no current mate.

Most of the parents of the young killers had been born in the South.[3] This is evident for 76.2% (16) of the 21 fathers and 48% (12) of the 25 mothers for whom information was available. The remaining parents had originated in Michigan, almost all in Detroit. It is interesting to note that every parent of a White subject for whom data were available (7 of the 10 White parents) had originated in the South. Perhaps Pettigrew and Spier's (1962) thesis that migration of Blacks from the nation's "last frontier" (the South, with its violent cultural tradition) is an important consideration in the causal complex of Black homicide and may apply to second-generation immigrants and to Whites as well. It is the contention of Pettigrew and Spier (1962) that Blacks reared in the Southern violent tradition who migrate to the bottom rungs of a new and threatening urban environment are prime candidates for offensive violence. However, the observation that only one-fourth of the 24 parents for whom information was recorded had a criminal record, and that the Southern-born were not over-represented among them, serve to weaken the Pettigrew-Spier hypothesis.

Reflective of the typically low socioeconomic status associated with homicide offenders (Wolfgang & Ferracuti, 1967, p. 261), this study population was characterized by families of relatively large size coupled with relatively low educational and occupational resources. The mothers of the 27 young offenders for whom data were available reportedly had a mean of 4 with a standard deviation of 1.9 living children. Only about half (51.3% or 20) of the 39 parents for whom information was recorded had completed high school, and less than half (47.1% or 16) of the 34 offenders for whom information was available resided with an employed custodian. Additionally, 44.8% (13) of the 29 killers for whom data were available were recipients of public welfare at the time of the offense.

Demographic and Social Relationships Between Offenders and Victims

Prior Social Relationships. Most reported killings in this country occur between persons who have had some prior relationship. Between 1980 and 1985 only 13.3% to 17.6% of homicides involved persons unknown to one another. In Detroit during the years 1982 and 1983, 19.1% of the 628 homicidal relationships[4] for which information has been recorded were categorized as "stranger." Among the present study population the proportion is somewhat larger. Over one-quarter (28.8% or 15) of the fifty-two decedents for whom information was available were slain by strangers. Nearly the same proportion (26.9% or 14) were each slain by friends and acquaintances, and 17.3% (9) were victimized by relatives (3 by sons, 4 by brothers, and 2 by cousins). The data describing prior social relationships between members of this young offender population and their victims indicate patterns basically consistent with those of age-general homicides.

Residential Relationship. In 14.5% (8) of the homicidal incidents perpetrated by this population of child arrestees, the offender and victim shared a residence at the time of the offense. From among those cases, four decedents (three males and a female) were slain by a brother, two fathers by a son, one male by a cousin, and one boarder by the son of his landlord.

Demographic Relationships: Race, Sex, and Age. This study indicates a proportion of intraracial killing as 76.3% (42) in total: 63.6% (35) of those cases were Black-on-Black, and the remaining 12.7% (7) were White-on-White. In all of those instances where members of the child population killed across racial lines

(20%[5] or 11), Blacks killed Whites. That fact is basically congruent with information describing the 1982–1983 age-general population of Detroit homicides, and with findings of the other homicide studies cited above, all of which demonstrate a higher proportion of Blacks killing Whites than vice versa. The 1982–1983 age-general data show that 6.4% of those deadly relationships were Black-on-White, and 2.1% were White-on-Black.

Homicide generally occurs between members of the same sex, and most of such intrasexual incidents involve males. Relatively few females kill, but when they do, their victims are almost always males (Bensing et al., 1960, pp. 57, 64; Block, 1976, p. 498; Gibbons, 1973, p. 36; Swigert & Farrell, 1978, p. 19; Voss & Hepburn, 1968, p. 503; Wilbanks, 1983a, p. 304; Wilbanks, 1983b, p. 10). In Detroit during 1982 and 1983, 66.4% of the 669 homicidal relationships for which information is available were intrasexual: 63.8% involved males, and the remaining 2.5% involved females. The study population of young killers demonstrates a higher proportion of intrasexual homicidal relationships, 83.6% (46) in total, with one case (1.8%) involving females. Frequencies associated with the two types of intersexual homicide for the young and the age-general Detroit populations clearly reflect the relatively low proportion of the young population constituting females. Whereas the two populations demonstrate very similar frequencies of male-on-female offenses (16.4% [9] and 15.7%, respectively), the child component shows no incidence of female-on-male homicide (compared with 17.9%).

In total, 67% (37) of the homicidal relationships perpetrated by the offenders under observation here involved a victim older than his slayer. This is a significantly higher proportion than the 45.2% associated with the 1982–1983 age-general Detroit homicide population. Furthermore, the mean difference in age between these young offenders and their victims was larger than that associated with the age-general population—18.2 years compared with 12.8 years. These data suggest that children who kill differ from their older counterparts both in degree and direction of age difference between them and their victims. They appear to select victims who deviate more from themselves in age, with that difference being in the direction of older.

Circumstances of Offense

General Social Context. The deadly encounters observed among this population of young offenders find their sources in a variety of contexts. While most (56.5% or 26) of the forty-six homicides for which information was reported were interpersonal acts of passion, a sizable proportion (21.7% or 10) were instrumental to the commission of another crime, and the same proportion were accidental (as determined by this researcher). Twenty-two adults (aged 19 and older) and twenty-six juveniles (including four infants aged 3 and younger) were killed in the forty-eight incidents, under the following circumstances:

1 adult and
11 juveniles were shot in the context of playing with guns in the home, and
1 juvenile while at school;
6 adults (in some cases peers, and in one case a father) and
6 juveniles were killed in the context of a quarrel;
10 adults were killed in the commission of robberies;
3 infants were killed by a babysitter;
2 adults (child's father, mother's boyfriend) were killed while beating the offender's mother;
1 infant was shot by another infant (both aged 3) while in the same bed;
1 juvenile and
1 adult (a peer) were shot in gang-related incidents;
1 adult roof repairman was shot as a result of being mistaken for an intruder;
1 juvenile and
1 adult were killed as a form of retaliation;
1 adult was shot in response to his son's anticipation of being beaten for receiving poor school grades; and
1 juvenile was killed as offender shot randomly into a cluster of school children.

Homicidal Method. Firearms are the most popular means of inflicting death in this country. Between 1968 and 1978 the proportion of homicides committed with firearms varied between 63% and 65.7% (Riedel, Zahn, & Mock, 1985, p. 48). In Detroit during 1982 and 1983, 65.8% of the 1,138 reported homicides were shootings. Of the remaining incidents, 17.8% were stabbings, 11.4% were beatings, 0.7% were burnings, and 4.2% were conducted by some other method. A somewhat smaller proportion, 58.3% (28), of fatal offenses perpetrated by this youthful population of Detroit killers were occasioned through use of firearms. Another 18.8% (9) each were stabbings and beatings, and 2.1% (1) consisted of each a burning and the inflicting of trauma resulting in a heart attack. It is of interest to note that among those thirty-seven homicides committed through use of a firearm or knife, nearly half (45.9% or 17) were effected while the perpetrator was carrying the weapon outside his home.

Number of Victims and Offenders. Most homicides are one-on-one incidents. Detroit provides no exception to this generalization, and neither do the young killers in that city. In Detroit during 1982 and 1983, 87.9% of the 578 homicides for which information is available were one-on-one offenses. Another 10.6% of those offenses were single victim/multiple offender; 1.4% were multiple victim/single offender; and the remaining 0.2% were multiple-victim/multiple-offender offenses. A slightly smaller proportion of the killings perpetrated by the young offenders observed here, 77% or 37, were one-on-one. The remaining portion of the killings were multiple offender/single victim in nature; 12.5% (6) involved two killers, 6.3% (3) involved three, and 4.2% (2) involved four. It should be noted that of the thirty-seven nonaccidental homicides for which data were available, 73% (27) were performed in the presence of at least one peer.

Victim Precipitation. Information on victim precipitation could be gleaned from police records of forty-five offenses perpetrated by this population of young Detroit killers. Nearly 16% (7) of those incidents were victim precipitated. This proportion is low when compared with studies of age-general homicide populations, which report victim precipitation to characterize between 22% and 37.9% of deadly disputes (Curtis, 1974, p. 83; Voss & Hepburn, 1968, p. 506; Wolfgang, 1958, p. 254).

Spatial Considerations. The present Detroit study suggests that child offenders are more likely to kill in a private residence setting than are their older counterparts. Nearly 69% (33) of the homicidal acts under observation here were accomplished in a home: 16.7% (8) occurred at the residence of the offender, 18:8% (9) at each the residence of the victim and the residence of both, and 14.6% (7) took place at another residence. The remaining incidents occurred on public streets (13 or 27.1%), in a commercial setting (1 or 2.1%), and at school (1 or 2.1%).

In total, 16% (5) of the thirty-one Detroit offenses committed at a private residence for which information was available occurred outside the acutal residence, usually on the porch or in the yard. Another 25.8% (8) occurred in the living room, 22.6% (7) in a bedroom, 6.5% (2) in the kitchen, 3.2% (1) in the bathroom, and 25.8% (8) in another room.

Temporal Considerations. For 1982 and 1983 combined, the frequency distribution of all Detroit homicides over the twelve months indicates a general overall stability except for slight increases during August–September and December–January, and a discernible dip in April. In comparison, the young study population demonstrated less stability, but showed some similar deviations. Like the age-general population, the youngsters effected an increase in August, where the frequency peaked out at 16.7% (8) of the forty-eight homicides, and in December, where the frequency followed up with 14.6% (7). Unlike the age-general population, however, the distribution for the young offenders showed extreme increases during March–April (14.6% [7] and 12.5% [6], respectively), and profound dips during May and July (2.1% [1] each).

Relative to days of week and hours of day, the young research population demonstrated some clear points of variation from the norm. Data are consistent in indicating that homicide is concentrated during weekends, but the young killers observed here provide an exception to that generalization. While studies of age-general homicide populations suggest that between 56.6% and 84% of deadly encounters occur on Fridays, Saturdays, and Sundays (the days with the three highest single frequencies), this population of young offenders accomplished only 41.6% (20) of their offenses on those three days. Compared with homicides perpetrated by age-general populations, those under consideration here are distributed more evenly throughout the week, with Friday reflecting the highest frequency (20.8% or 10) and Saturday the lowest (8.3% or 3).

Congruous with the age-general homicide populations, the young Detroit offenders effected approximately three-quarters (70.8% or 34) of their homicides between 2:00 P.M. and 1:59 A.M. But unlike the age-general populations, they committed a lower proportion (22.9% or 11) between 8:00 P.M. and 1:59 A.M. than between 2:00 P.M. and 7:59 P.M. (47.9% or 23).

DISCUSSION

The construction of a statistical profile describing the population of 55 individuals under age 15 who were arrested for homicide in the predominantly Black city of Detroit, Michigan, for offenses perpetrated between 1977 and 1984 yields the image of a 12- or 13-year-old Black male, born and currently living in Detroit with only one of his natural parents in a single-family residential unit that currently houses a total of four or five persons. He has changed residential guardianship at least once in his life, and the killing that predisposed him to this study population represents his first official police contact. Though he is legitimately born, his parents are no longer married and living together; his father is remarried, and his mother is single. His parents are Southern born, with relatively large families and limited educational and occupational resources. The deadly incident was an act of passion involving a friend, acquaintance, or relative who also was a Black male, was fifteen years his senior, and with whom he did not share living quarters. This homicidally aggressive child was the first to effect physical force in the homicide drama that culminated in a fatal gunshot in a private residence on a Tuesday, Thursday, or Friday between 2:00 P.M. and 1:59 A.M.

It appears from this Detroit study population that while children are subject generally to homicidal patterns characteristic of their older counterparts, they perhaps deviate somewhat from those norms along certain dimensions. Their offenses more commonly may be interracial, specifically Black-on-White, and more likely to involve males as both perpetrators and victims. They may select victims who are more different from themselves in age, with that difference being in the direction of older. A higher proportion of violent deaths effected by these youngsters may victimize strangers, may be inflicted through stabbings and beatings, and may occur in a private residence. They may be more evenly distributed over the days of the week.

One noteworthy observation associated with these data relates to the thirteen deaths—representing over one-quarter of the total victims—resulting from gun play. This finding lends clear support to the relentless and highly controversial arguments directed toward firearm control in this country (Zimring, 1968). While means to intervention of unintended shootings by children have been identified, the trend appears to be not toward reducing the problem, but toward aggravating it by the recent production of lightweight (made largely of plastic) and inexpensive handguns. These weapons are designed to be particularly attractive to women to use in self-defense, and resemble toys even more closely than do their predecessors (Wintemute, Teret, Kraus, Wright, & Bradfield, 1987).

NOTES

1. Actually, some subjects are not arrestees. They were "known" by police to have perpetrated the homicide, but were not taken into cus-

tody because of their age. For the purpose of this study, however, they are not distinguished from the arrestees.

2. These data were selected for comparison because of their availability. They had been computed by this author for a previous study (Goetting, 1992).

3. Using the geographic grouping of states adopted by the U.S. Bureau of the Census, the South includes Delaware, Maryland, District of Columbia, Virginia, West Virginia, North Carolina, South Carolina, Georgia, Florida, Kentucky, Tennessee, Alabama, Mississippi, Arkansas, Louisiana, Oklahoma, and Texas.

4. Throughout this section entitled "Demographic and Social Relationships Between Offenders and Victims," the data describing homicidal relationships characteristic of the age-general 1982–1983 Detroit homicide population take into consideration all relationships associated with not only single-offender/single-victim killings, but also with multiple-offender and/or multiple-victim offenses. This means that the number of homicidal relationships associated with a certain analysis is greater than the number of actual homicides involved. The study population data on child killers with which these age-general data are compared include information on homicidal relationships involving child offenders only. The eleven older killers who were co-offenders in eight of the homicidal incidents perpetrated by the young offenders are excluded from these comparative analyses of demographic and social homicidal relationships.

5. For the purpose of this analysis, racial categories are limited to include White and Black. Consequently, the 3.6% (2) of the cases that involved "other-on-other" offenses are excluded. This explains why the 20% of interracial and the 76.3% of interracial offenses fail to constitute a full 100% of the homicides.

The Elderly Offender

Introduction to Part VI

Elderly Americans are at low risk of perpetrating homicides when compared with all other age categories except young children. This is in keeping with the relationship between age of offender and crime in general (Daly & Wilson, 1990, pp. 90–91). There is some indication that demographic, behavioral, and circumstantial patterns of homicide vary with age of offender, and that those patterns persist across gender lines (Block, 1990). Therefore, when considering homicide events perpetrated by older Americans, the image is one of distinct pattern coupled with relatively infrequent occurrence. Chapter 9, "Patterns of Homicide Among the Elderly," profiles the Detroit homicide offender age 55 and older. Accumulated research on this subject, including four additional recent profiles (Block, 1990, p. 60; Gilbert, 1992; Kratcoski, 1993; Silverman & Kennedy, 1993, pp. 166–175 [Canada]) have established a somewhat predictable scenario.

Patterns of Homicide Among the Elderly

9

While much research attention has been devoted to the elderly as victims of violence, very little is understood concerning them as violent offenders. This study attempts to modify that knowledge gap by observing homicide offenders in the contexts of their deadly acts.

To date, only two studies have addressed directly the subject of older killers. Wilbanks and Murphy (1984) and Kratcoski and Walker (1988) conducted comparative analyses of arrestees for criminal homicide aged 60 and over and their younger counterparts. Wilbanks and Murphy (1984) used the F.B.I.'s Supplemental Homicide Report data for their 1980 nationwide study, and Kratcoski and Walker (1988) used cases recorded in the coroner's office of Cuyahoga County, Ohio for the years 1970–1983. While these research endeavors provide valuable insights into deadly events perpetrated by the elderly, depth of information is severly limited by their data bases. It is the purpose of this research to complement and extend these two studies with more-detailed accounts of circumstances surrounding homicidal activities performed by older Americans. Specifically, this work is a response to Shichor and Kobrin's (1978, p. 215) observation that "Little information is available with regard to the settings in which violence among the elderly occurs, the weapons or other means employed, and the character of the victims."

The analyses outlined in these pages constitute a descriptive account of homicides perpetrated by elderly persons in a Northern city during 1982 and 1983. Since many of the variables included in the analyses have been dealt with in earlier homicide studies that based their findings almost entirely on cases involving nonelderly offenders, cursory comparisons of deadly encounters involving elderly and nonelderly perpetrators are possible. The material is presented through use of the four-part organizational scheme.

RESEARCH METHODS

The subjects selected for this study include all arrestees[1] connected with homicides (except those attributed to the negligent use of a vehicle) committed in the city of Detroit, Michigan, during 1982 and 1983 who were 55 years of age or older[2] at the time of the offense. As in other studies described in this work, a limitation of this study lies in its lack of generalizability; its subjects are drawn from an urban, predominantly Black population with an inordinately high homicide rate. The study population includes a total of 45 offenders associated with the slaying of 49 victims. These 45 offenders represent 6.5% of all homicide arrestees in that city during those two years. Data collection took place on June 20 and 21, 1984, in the offices of the Homicide Section of the Detroit Police Department. Police-recorded information regarding each case, including the Investigator's Report, Interrogation Record, and Witness Statements was electronically copied for subsequent perusal.

Data on all sociologically relevant variables that could be gleaned from the material were coded and tabulated. When feasible, comparisons are made with the total population of Detroit arrestees for homicides committed during 1982 and 1983, and with previous homicide studies that did not control for age, and therefore based their findings nearly totally on cases involving nonelderly offenders. Since the proportion of homicide arrestees aged 55 and older consistently hovers near 5% (Shichor, 1984,

p. 23), this means that the comparisons employed should have, according to the laws of probability, utilized populations and samples constituting approximately 95% members younger than 55 years of age. Clearly the comparisons applied for this study are less than ideal on two counts: (1) the comparison groups are not mutually exclusive for the offender age and (2) except when 1982 and 1983 Detroit data are available, the comparison groups are not geographically and temporally comparable.

RESULTS

Demographic Characteristics of Offenders and Victims

The study population of offenders ranged in age between 55 and 82 years, with a mean of 64.5 years (SD=7.3). Their victims were in general considerably younger, ranging from 8 to 92 years of age, with a mean of 42.3 years (SD=20.3).

Research repeatedly has verified that homicide offenders and their victims are disproportionately Black. Detroit provides no exception to this generalization, and neither do the older killers in that city. In 1980, 63% of the Detroit population was Black (U.S. Bureau of the Census, 1983). Of all arrestees for homicides committed there during the years 1982 and 1983, 89.1% were Black, and 81.9% of victims were Black. Data revealed that while about the same proportion of elderly arrestees were Black (88.9% or 40), a somewhat higher proportion of their victims (93% or 46) were of that racial category. These data suggest that while older killers are racially similar to their younger counterparts, they are somewhat more likely to select Blacks as their victims.

Homicide offenders and victims are disproportionately male, and, again, Detroit data are consistent with that generalization. Approximately 82% of the 1982–83 age-general population of Detroit homicide arrestees were male, as were 77.2% of slain victims during those same years in that city. Among the elderly constituent of that population, 88.9% (40) of offenders and 83.7% (41) of their victims were male. Data describing these Detroit homicides suggest that a somewhat higher proportion of elderly than nonelderly offenders and their victims were male. These findings are consistent with Shichor's (1985, p. 406) data indicating that the ratio of male-to-female homicide offenders among the elderly was higher than the ratio of younger-male-to-younger-female homicide offenders. They are inconsistent, however, with Kratcoski and Walker's (1988, p. 71) observation of no change in the ratio of male-to-female homicide from the 15–59 age bracket to the 60-and-older age bracket.

Of the 40 arrestees for whom marital status was available, most (70% or 28) were unmarried or separated from their spouses at the time of the killing. The remaining 30% (12) were residing with their legal or common-law spouses. Information on domestic status was available for only 23 of the 49 victims. Probably because they were younger than their slayers, a higher proportion (43.5% or 10) was residing with spouses, leaving 47.8% (11) unmarried adults and 8.7% (2) below the age of 15 and therefore categorized as children.

Of the 30 offenders for whom information on formal education was available, 53.3% (16) had completed at least eight years of school, and 20% (6) had completed at least 12 years. One had completed 13 years, and another, 16 years. These data reflect a relatively low level of formal education when compared with the general United States population in the same age category at the same point in time.[3] They are consistent with Swigert and Farrell's (1978, p. 193) finding that nearly three-quarters of homicide offenders had less than a high school education and with other studies (Bensing, Schroeder, & Jackson, 1960, pp. 128–29; Wolfgang, 1958, pp. 36–39) suggesting that such offenders are concentrated in the lower social classes.

Employment information was available for 38 of the elderly arrestees in the study population. Only 21.1% (8) of them were gainfully employed at the time of the offense; the rest were retired or otherwise unemployed. While unemployment has been shown to be associated with homicide in the general population (Munford et al., 1976, pp. 228–29), that association loses its meaning with this elderly sample due to retirement practices in this country.

Residence and Family Network of Offender. All elderly arrestees and their victims for whom data were available (44 and 46, respectively) were residing in the city of Detroit at the time of the offense. Most (54.5% or 24) of the 44 killers for whom information was available lived with family member(s) and/or lover(s) at the time of the offense. Nearly 14% (6) resided with unrelated person(s), and the remaining 31.8% (14) lived alone.

Most research offenders reported having living family members. Of the 29 subjects for whom information was available, 17.2% (5) reported having a mother and 10.3% (3) reported having a father. Of the 31 killers who supplied information on siblings, 83.9% (26) reported at least one to be living, and of the 32 for whom information on children was available, 68.8% (22) reported at least one to be living.

Arrest Record of Offender. Detroit Police Department arrest records[4] indicate that nearly three-fourths (72.7% or 32) of the 44 elderly offenders for whom data were available had been arrested in that city before the homicides that predisposed them to the study population. While this is a crude measure of criminal history, since it is limited to police activity within the perimeter of a single city and since it fails to delineate the particular charges and dispositions associated with arrests, it does suggest that a high proportion of the older killers under observation here are likely to have had criminal backgrounds. Available research indicates that when these elderly offenders are compared with age-general populations of homicide offenders, their proportion having experienced previous arrests is relatively high. Wolfgang (1958, p. 175) reports 64% and Swigert and Farrell (1978, p. 194) report 56% of their homicide offender populations as having had previous arrest records. The inflated proportion of 72.7% associated with this elderly population may well be a simple artifact of time, however. Older offenders incur greater risk for arrest by virtue of age alone.

***Social and Demographic Relationships between Offenders
and Victims.*** Most reported killings in this country occur between persons having had some prior relationship. Between 1980
and 1985 only 13.3% to 17.6% of homicides involved persons unknown to one another. In Detroit during the years 1982 and 1983,
19.1% of the 628 homicidal relationships[5] for which information
has been recorded were categorized as "strangers." Among the
elderly offenders the proportion is somewhat larger. Just under
one-quarter (24.5% or 12) of the 49 decedents under consideration in this study were slain by strangers. Another 18.4% (9) were
killed by offenders in each of the three following relationship
categories: spouses or romantic acquaintances, other relatives,
and casual acquaintances. An additional 20.4% (10) were killed
by unrelated housemates or roommates or by platonic friends.
The data describing prior social relationships between members
of this older offender population and their victims indicate patterns basically consistent with those of age-general homicides.
One lucid reflection of that consistency lies in the fact that all
five women in the population perpetrated domestic killings,[6] in
these cases all involving spouses or lovers.

It is of interest to note that the findings of this Detroit study as
they relate to offender–victim relationship are inconsonant with
those of Wilbanks and Murphy (1984, pp. 84–85) and Kratcoski
and Walker (1988, p. 70). In Detroit, a higher proportion of older
homicide arrestees selected strangers as victims than did the
comparable age-general population (24.5%) and 19.1%, respectively). The other studies, however, demonstrate the opposite
trend; those researchers found that elderly homicide arrestees
were only about half as likely to have killed strangers than were
their nonelderly counterparts (7.7% and 16.5%, respectively, for
Wilbanks & Murphy and 10% and 17%, respectively, for Kratcoski & Walker).

For approximately one-quarter (26.5% or 13) of the homicidal
incidents perpetrated by this population of arrestees, the offender
and victim shared a residence at the time of the offense. From
among those cases, five decedents (three men and two women)
were slain by a spouse or cohabitant, two sons by a father, one

man by a brother, one man by a stepfather, and four men by unrelated housemates or roommates.

Homicide offenders and their victims are nearly always of the same race (Woodrum, 1990). In Detroit during 1982 and 1983, 91.4% of the 669 homicidal relationships for which information is available were intraracial; 82.7% were Black-on-Black, and the remaining 8.7% were White-on-White. This study indicates that a slightly higher proportion of the elderly component of that offender population, 93.9% (46), killed within racial boundaries; 87.8% (43) of those cases were Black-on-Black, and the remaining, 6.1% (3) were White-on-White. In all of those instances where the elderly killed across racial lines (6.1% or 3), Whites killed Blacks. That fact is incongruent with information describing the general population of Detroit homicides during that time period and with findings of the other homicide studies cited above, all of which demonstrate a higher proportion of Blacks killing Whites than vice versa. The 1982–83 age-general Detroit homicide data show that 6.4% of those deadly incidents were Black-on-White, and 2.1% were White-on-Black. It is of interest to note that these Detroit homicide data describing the racial relationship between elderly offender and victim are consistent with those of Wilbanks and Murphy (1984, pp. 85–86), who report that a slightly higher proportion of the elderly than nonelderly offenders in their nationwide population killed intraracially.

Homicide generally occurs between members of the same sex, and nearly all of such intrasexual incidents involve men. Relatively few women kill, and when they do, their victims are almost always men (Woodrum, 1990). In Detroit during 1982 and 1983, 66.4% of the 669 reported homicidal relationships were intrasexual; 63.8% involved men, and the remaining 2.5% involved women. The elderly component of that population demonstrates a somewhat higher proportion of intrasexual homicidal relationships, 73.5% (36), and all involving men. Frequencies associated with the two types of intersexual homicide for the elderly and the age-general Detroit populations clearly reflect the relatively low proportion of the elderly population constituting women. Whereas the two populations demonstrate very similar frequencies of male-on-female offenses (16.3% (8) and 15.7%, respectively), the older component shows a relatively small proportion of female-on-male offenses (10.2% or 5 compared with 17.9%).

Eighty-three percent (40) of the 48 homicidal relationships for which information was available involved a victim younger than his or her slayer. This is a significantly higher proportion than the 47.5% associated with the comparable age-general population. Furthermore, the mean difference in age between elderly offenders and their victims was nearly double that of the age-general population—25 years compared with 12.8 years. These data suggest that elderly killers may differ from their younger counterparts in terms of both degree and direction of age difference between them and their victims. Clearly they select victims who are more different from themselves in age, with that difference being in the direction of younger. This observation is consistent with the findings of Wilbanks and Murphy (1984, pp. 87–88).

CIRCUMSTANCES OF OFFENSE

Homicidal Motive and Method

In the current study, nearly one-third (32.7% or 16) of the 49 offenses resulted from domestic quarrels, and a slightly higher proportion, 34.7% (17), originated in arguments with friends, neighbors, and acquaintances. Another 20.4% (10) were responses to some form of criminal threat or victimization, 2% (1) arose from an altercation with a stranger, and 4.1% (2) were alleged accidents. Finally, 6.1% (3) are best described as psychotic reactions.

As noted in earlier chapters, firearms are the most common means of inflicting death in this country. In Detroit during 1982 and 1983, 65.8% of the 1138 reported homicides were shootings. Another 17.8% were stabbings, 11.4% were beatings, 0.7% were burnings, and 4.2% were conducted by some other means. A somewhat larger proportion, 79.6% (39), of homicides perpetrated by the elderly component of Detroit killers during those years was carried out through use of firearms. Additionally, 8.2% (4) each were stabbings and beatings, and the remaining 4.1% (2) were burnings. These data are inconsistent with the findings of Kratcoski and Walker (1988, p. 72), who discovered no significant difference by age in homicidal method: 88% of the young and 89% of the old offenders selected firearms. The results of the Wilbanks and Murphy (1984, p. 88) study, however, are consistent with these Detroit data. Those researchers report a statistically significant difference in homicidal method when comparing their elderly and nonelderly offenders. The older killers were shown to have used firearms in 78.1%, knives in 12.4%, and other weapons in 9.4% of their offenses, while comparable proportions for their nonelderly counterparts were 63.3%, 20.9% and 15.8%. Both the Detroit and the Wilbanks and Murphy (1984, p. 88) data support the hypothesis of Wilbanks and Murphy (1984, p. 88) that older and presumably weaker persons are more likely to select firearms to compensate for lack of physical strength.

Number of Victims and Offenders

Almost all homicides are one-on-one incidents. Detroit provides no exception to this generalization, and neither do the older killers in that city. In Detroit during 1982 and 1983, 87.9% of the 578 homicides for which information is available involved a single victim and a single offender. Another 10.6% of those offenses were single-victim/multiple-offender; 1.4% were multiple-victim/single-offender; and the remaining 0.2% were multiple-victim/multiple-offender offenses. A slightly larger proportion of the killings perpetrated by the elderly offenders involved a single victim and offender. Over 91% (41) of those incidents were characterized by such simplicity. The remaining offenses were distributed in the following manner: 1.2% (1) were single-victim/multiple-offender; 4.4% (2) were multiple-victim/single-offender; and another 2.2% (1) were multiple-victim/multiple-offender. Wilbanks and Murphy's (1984, p. 87) comparative analyses yield results consistent with these Detroit data. Their findings support their hypothesis that elderly homicide offenders would more likely perpetrate single-offender homicide events than would their younger counterparts. They reason that most multiple-offender killings are incidental to some felony-related activity such as robbery and burglary on the part of the principals, and because the elderly are less likely to be engaged in such criminal activities, they are less likely to be perpetrators of such slayings. It is of interest to note, consistent with the assumption of Wilbanks and Murphy (1984, p. 87), that for none of the 49 killings executed by this elderly research population was the slaying incidental to the commitment of another crime by the offender.

Victim Precipitation

Information on victim precipitation could be gleaned from 1982 and 1983 Detroit police records for 46 offenses perpetrated by individuals aged 55 and older. Nearly 35% (16) of those incidents were victim precipitated. This proportion is congruent with data from studies of age-general homicide populations, which report victim precipitation to characterize between 22% and 37.9% of homicides (Curtis, 1974, p. 83; Voss & Hepburn, 1968, p. 506; Wolfgang, 1958, p. 254). It should be noted that four of the five offenses perpetrated by women were victim precipitated. This observation is consistent with Wolfgang's (1958, p. 255) finding that females were twice as frequently offenders in victim-precipitated slayings (29%) as they were in non-victim-precipitated killings (14%).

Spatial and Temporal Considerations

This Detroit study suggests that older offenders are more likely to kill in the residential setting than are their younger counterparts. Nearly four-fifths (78.7% or 37) of the 47 homicidal acts for which data were available were accomplished in a home: 44.7% (21) occurred at the residence of the offender, 4.3% (2) at the residence of the victim, 25.5% (12) at the residence of both, and 4.3% (2) at another residence. Of the remaining incidents, 6.4% (3) took place on public streets, 2.1% (1) in a bar, 8.5% (4)

in other commercial places, and 4.3% (2) in empty privately owned buildings. These data are consistent with Kratcoski and Walker's (1988, p. 69) finding that while approximately half of homicides perpetrated by nonelderly assailants took place in the home, more than two-thirds involving their elderly counterparts occurred there. It should be noted that all five women in the Detroit research population performed their homicidal acts at private residences. This difference between women and men is consistent with data reported by Wolfgang (1958, p. 124) and later by Swigert and Farrell (1978, p. 199), indicating that a higher proportion of women offenders kill at home.

Nearly one-third (31.4% or 11) of the 35 Detroit offenses committed at a private residence for which information was available occurred outside the actual residence, usually on the porch or in the yard. Another 22.9% (8) occurred in a bedroom, 17.1% (6) in the living room, and 14.3% (5) in each the kitchen and another room.

The elderly study population demonstrates an overall stability in homicide frequency across the months but with different deviations. There was no irregularity in frequency during the holiday season, and August alone marked an extremely divergent peak (16.3% or 8, with the next highest proportion in the 12-month distribution being 10.2% or 5). Congruent with the age-general population of killings, there was a lull during April, but unlike the age-general distribution, there was a profound dip in June.

Relative to days of week and hours of day, the elderly research population demonstrated some interesting points of variation from the norm. Data are consistent in indicating that homicide is concentrated during weekends (Bensing et al., 1960, p. 11; Voss & Hepburn, 1968, p. 504; Wolfgang, 1958, p. 107), and these elderly offenders provide no exception to that generalization. But while studies of age-general homicide populations suggest that between 56.6% and 84% of deadly encounters occur on Fridays, Saturdays, and Sundays (the days with the three highest single frequencies), this population of older killers accomplished only half (24) of their 48 offenses for which information was available on those three days. Congruent with the norm, Saturday reflects the highest frequency for them (27.1% or 13), but inconsistent with age-general homicide populations, Monday ranks a close second, representing one-fourth (12) of all fatal assaults. Furthermore, for the elderly Detroit population, the frequency of offenses associated with Sunday is relatively low at 8.3% (4). To some extent, the elderly population displayed violent behavior on Mondays typical of Sunday behavior in the age-general population.

Wolfgang (1958, p. 108) and Pokorney (1965, p. 482) provide the only two sources of information that can be compared directly with data describing these older Detroit killers on the subject of time of offense.[7] The two studies are consistent with one another in indicating that approximately half of homicides occur between 8:00 P.M. and 1:59 A.M., and another quarter occur between 2:00 P.M. and 7:59 P.M. Congruous with age-general homicide populations, the elderly Detroit offenders executed three-quarters (36) of the 48 homicides for which information was available between 2:00 P.M. and 1:59 A.M. But unlike the age-general populations, they committed a lower proportion (35.4% or 17) between 8:00 P.M. and 1:59 A.M. than between 2:00 P.M. and 7:59 P.M. (39.6% or 19).

ARREST DISPOSITION

Several studies (Bachand, 1983; Cutshall & Adams, 1983; Dickens, 1969; Feinberg & McGriff, 1986; Lindquist & White, 1987; Wilbanks, 1988) probe the question of prosecutorial leniency based on advanced age, with mixed results. Of the 44 applicable members of this Detroit research population (excluding the homicide-suicide case), 45.5% (20) were denied warrant for criminal charge by the Prosecuting Attorney. This suggests leniency when compared with the estimated 30.4% of the general population of homicide arrestees for that city during 1983 who were similarly denied warrant.[8] Further analyses controlling for severity of crime and other factors are necessary in order to appropriately pursue the question of prosecutorial leniency toward elderly homicide offenders.

Court dispositions relating to the 24 Detroit arrestees who were issued warrants for criminal charges indicate that half (12) were convicted of Murder or Manslaughter; 8.3% (2) were convicted of Possession of a Firearm During Commission of a Felony (a felony); 12.5% (3) were convicted of a misdemeanor including Careless Discharge and Intentionally Pointing a Firearm Without Malice; 25% (6) were acquitted; and 4.2% (1) were awaiting court disposition at this writing. Of the 18 convicted arrestees, nearly three-fourths (72.2% or 13) received prison sentences. The determination of one sentence was postponed indefinitely while the defendant remained committed to a mental institution. Not surprisingly, all of the subjects who were convicted of Murder or Manslaughter received a prison sentence (except the man who was committed to a mental institution).

CONCLUSIONS

The construction of a statistical profile describing the population of 45 individuals aged 55 and older who were arrested for homicide in the predominantly Black city of Detroit, Michigan, for offenses perpetrated during 1982 and 1983 yields the image of a currently unmarried Black male with an eighth- or ninth-grade education who is retired or otherwise unemployed. He lives in Detroit with at least one family member or a lover. While his parents are deceased, he claims at least one living sibling and offspring. He had an arrest record with the Detroit Police Department prior to the fatal encounter that predisposed him to the study population. That deadly incident erupted from a domestic quarrel or an argument with a friend, neighbor, or acquaintance who also was a Black male, was approximately 22 years his junior, and with whom he did not share living quarters. This older killer was the first to apply physical force in the homicide drama that culminated in a fatal gunshot in a private residence on a Friday, Saturday, or Monday between 2:00 P.M. and 1:59 A.M.

In many important ways elderly homicide offenders appear to be indistinguishable from their younger counterparts. But they do seem to deviate from the norm along certain dimensions, and some of these deviations provide clues to understanding the relatively low proportion of older people in this country who kill (Shichor, 1984, pp. 18, 23; Wilbanks & Murphy, 1984, p. 81). Consider first the age relationship between offender and victim. Information reported herein suggests that the general population of homicide offenders selects victims who are more normally and closely distributed around their own age than do older killers, who commonly victimize persons much younger than themselves. Apparently, killing is something that in general is done to near-agemates. Perhaps so few older people kill partly because their high-risk category of potential victims in terms of age has been reduced by natural attrition. Location of offense may be another explanatory variable. Research suggests that when compared with their younger counterparts, older killers commit proportionally fewer offenses outside a private residence. Perhaps older people, due to various factors including fear of criminal victimization (LaGrange & Ferraro, 1989), spend less time in public and commercial places and more time at home and in the homes of family members, friends, and casual acquaintances. This, of course, would place them at lower risk of killing outside the home where approximately half of homicides occur.

Another factor that may contribute insight into the under-representation of the elderly among homicide offenders is time of offense. Proportionally fewer homicides perpetrated by older persons appear to be committed between 8:00 P.M. and 1:59 A.M. For some reason, the elderly are less inclined to kill late at night than are the nonelderly. Perhaps they retire to bed earlier in the evening. And perhaps they are likely to withdraw to private quarters for fear of criminal victimization, as suggested above, at an earlier hour. This would place them at reduced risk for involvement in that high proportion of violence that occurs late at night in bars and other recreational sites conducive to homicide. It should be noted that if these spatial and temporal restrictions are, in fact, characteristic of the generalized lifestyle of the elderly, that may help to explain why a slightly higher proportion of these elderly offenders, compared with their age-general counterparts, killed within racial boundaries. If older people spend more time in their own homes and those of family, friends, and neighbors, they are at lower risk of encountering members of other racial categories.

One last explanatory consideration suggested by these data is rooted in homicidal method. Available information indicates that while elderly and nonelderly killers alike select firearms as the most common means of inflicting death, a somewhat higher proportion of the elderly do so. Perhaps older people are less likely to kill than are their younger counterparts at least in part because they need an available firearm to do so. And many, for whatever reasons—practical, financial, moral, cultural (i.e., women and adherents to certain religious beliefs are socialized not to use guns)—have no such weapon handy when the homicidal urge occurs.

There is one remaining factor, external to the variables examined in this analysis, that may contribute significantly to the low incidence of killings perpetrated by elderly Americans: that is a selection factor. Perhaps the proportion of homicidal elderly is reduced by the relatively high attrition rate over the life span of violent individuals. Persons with predispositions toward violence (due to biosocial,[9] personality, or cultural antecedents) are probably less likely to reach the age of 55 years and to therefore be at risk of committing geriatric homicide.

When considered together, all of these explanatory factors suggest that the social location of the elderly and their corresponding lifestyle may structure the nature of their criminality. A more general observation along these lines has been articulated by Cohen and Felson (1979) in their application of the human ecological theory to criminal behavior. Their "routine activity approach to explaining criminal behavior assumes criminal inclination, then proceeds to examine the manner in which the spatio-temporal organization of social activities helps people to translate their criminal inclinations into action." Criminal violations are viewed as routine activities that share many attributes, and are interdependent of, other routine activities. They occur because of social-structural opportunities. Perhaps the elderly perpetrate less homicide because their place in the social structure is less conducive to such activity.

This study provides a highly detailed account of a subject about which we know very little, but it is severly limited in that its findings are not generalizable. Since generalizability is critical to social-scientific inquiry, the next step along this analytical path would be to collaborate to the extent possible these Detroit finding with a 1982–1983 national data set, specifically with Supplemental Homicide Report data. To the extent that the findings related to variables common to these two data sets (single/multiple victim/offender; age, sex, race, ethnic origin of victim and offender; weapon; personal relationship; and circumstances) show consistency (rendering those Detroit findings generalizable), we can operate, in the absence of contrary evidence, under the assumption that the Detroit findings related to the other variables (domestic status; education; employment status; residence; family network; arrest record; shared residence; victim precipitation; spatial and temporal considerations; and arrest disposition) are also generalizable.

NOTES

1. Actually, one subject is not an arrestee: he is a homicide/suicide case, so was never arrested. For the purpose of this study, however, he is not distinguished from the arrestees.

2. For the purpose of studying law-breaking behavior, 55 years of age generally has been accepted as the lower cut-off point for the "elderly age" category. This designation is suggested by Shichor and Kobrin (1978), who discovered that arrest statistics indicate a significant drop at this point in the age distribution.

3. In March of 1982, 83.8% of noninstitutionalized people in this country aged 55 and older had completed eight years of formal education, and 53.1% had completed four years of high school. In 1983, comparable proportions were 84.5% and 54.3% (U.S. Bureau of the Census, 1982–83).

4. A special search for arrest information relating to members of the study population was conducted in December of 1984 by Inspector John

A. Clark of the Information Systems Section of the Detroit Department of Police.

5. Throughout this section entitled Demographic and Social Relationships Between Offenders and Victims, the data describing homicidal relationships characteristic of the age-general 1982–83 Detroit homicide population take into consideration all relationships associated with not only single-offender/single-victim killings, but also with multiple-offender and/or multiple-victim offenses. This means that the number of homicidal relationships associated with a certain analysis is greater than the number of actual homicides involved. The elderly research population data with which these age-general data are compared include information on homicidal relationships involving elderly offenders only. The three nonelderly killers who were co-offenders in two of the homicidal incidents perpetrated by members of the elderly study population are excluded from these comparative analyses of demographic and social homicidal relationships.

6. Prior research has demonstrated that female offenders are nearly always involved in domestic homicides (Wilbanks, 1983a, p. 304).

7. Only those two studies utilized a coding scheme for hour of offense similar to that employed for the present study.

8. The computation of this estimate can be found in an earlier Detroit homicide study conducted by Goetting (1988a).

9. A review of the biosocial or neurological antecedents of interpersonal violence was conducted by Elliott (1988).

Conclusion: Some
Preventive Considerations

The chapters assembled in this volume demonstrate the diversity in relational and social-structural context that can produce homicide. Each of the nine profiles represents a unique set of patterned demographics, behaviors, and circumstances that calls for a particular response system. Risk groups and risk factors vary among the profiles, but three risk factors surface as clear constants, not only among these Detroit studies, but throughout homicide research as well.

The first is poverty. Evidence of a positive relationship between poverty and homicide has persisted in the literature in studies of both homicide offenders and homicide rates. Poverty is a structural factor associated with the killing of friends and acquaintances, children, and spouses and with robbery-associated murders of strangers. One study finds poverty to be more strongly associated with murders of family members and friends than murders of acquaintances (Parker, 1989). Poverty may be the most important predictor of primary homicide (Parker, 1989, p. 999). All social-class indicators examined in this volume point to relative economic deprivation. The subjects of this Detroit research are characterized by low levels of formal education, high unemployment rates, and high rates of welfare dependency. Comparatively large proportions report that they are without residential telephones. The tentacles of poverty permeate the fabric of a

155

social structure to produce agonies of multiple dimensions. Somewhere immersed in the quagmire of poverty's despair erupts the homicide seed. One important site of that eruption, I concur with James Gilligan (1991), is in shame and humiliation. It must be emphasized that it is not poverty per se that affects the sometimes deadly consequences of shame and humiliation; rather, it is relative deprivation. It is the realization that one is the object of ridicule, degradation, oppression, and exploitation, that incites a person to establish or restore respect and ultimately self-respect through what may appear to him or her to be the only avenue— violence. Respect is critical to the well-being of humanity. Without it, psychological death is imminent; one will lapse into madness. Respect is the single life-element for which people will sacrifice all else (Gilligan, 1991). This point was introduced to criminology in 1977, when David Luckenbill reported that much homicide results from a confrontation in which at least one party attempts to establish or "save face" at the expense of others by "standing steady" or "demonstrating character." In contexts of both specific confrontational incidents ("Luckenbill killings") and general relative deprivation, homicide can represent a desperate attempt to claim or reclaim the sense of human dignity requisite to psychological survival. Gilligan (1991, pp. 16–17) explains:

> Shame motivates hostility toward others, which is usually limited to hostile thoughts and feelings but can culminate in hostile behavior as well, escalating to violence when nothing else is perceived as being capable of rescuing self-esteem or national honor. The purpose of violence is to restore and maintain respect for oneself or the social group with which one has identified (family, class, race, ethnic group, religion, nation) when the self or the group is perceived as having been shamed, insulted, or treated with disrespect. People need a certain minimal sense of pride and dignity, since to be overwhelmed by feelings of personal or national shame and humiliation is experienced psychologically as tantamount to the disintegration or death of the self or (what amounts to the same thing) of the group one has identified oneself with; and it is characteristically accompanied by the feeling, and the fear, of that dissolution of the self termed (by people going through the experience) "going crazy."

There are avenues to respect that are far superior to violence, but they generally are less accessible to the underprivileged classes. It is at least partly for this reason that homicide is over-represented among the poor. Gilligan (1991, pp. 18-19) continues:

> It is true that creating, achieving, or producing things that are valued by other people can command respect and lead to honors, prestige, status, wealth, and power, and that this can be an equally effective and even more permanent means for warding off ridi-cule than violent behavior can . . . [T]he experience of competing successfully, or achieving enough to attain one's level of ambition or aspiration, can heal the wounds to self-esteem that shame con-sists of. Unfortunately, achievement and creativity require time, patience, talent, education, and some minimal degree of social and economic advantage, as well as sheer good luck; and many people, and many peoples, have not had such fortunate combinations of both internal and external resources—whereas violence always lies ready at hand (literally).

Our nation is hemorrhaging from the inadvertent neglect of its own people. One consequence of that neglect is poverty, with its attendant sensations of shame and humiliation and the some-times resultant violence. A task before the public health commu-nity is to align this linkage between poverty and homicide with appropriate interventive strategy. The goal must be nothing less than social and economic reform designed to guarantee as a birth-right to all Americans standards of employment, education, health, and housing that will command interpersonal respect and universal dignity. Preventive intervention would begin with the unborn child in the form of support to expectant parents. Chil-dren can thrive and develop into responsible and respectable contributors to our social and economic order only if their par-ents feel valued and supported in their domestic roles. As a nation, we can afford to implement the programs and policies shown effective in reducing poverty (Goetting, 1994) and, in turn, in operating as agents in the primary prevention of homicide.

The second risk factor identified from these Detroit studies that is generally recognized in the research literature is firearm abuse, which is strongly associated with all profiles except those describing child victims and females against females. Firearm abuse is an important homicide risk factor in this nation; about 60% of homicides are committed with guns (Reiss & Roth, 1993, p. 255).

Firearms are widely owned and widely accessible in the U.S. (Reiss & Roth, 1993, p. 256). The estimated national gun population for 1990 is 200 million; about 50% of all households own at least one firearm. Gun ownership is not uniform throughout the population. The fraction of households owning firearms is greatest in rural areas and small towns, higher for Whites than for Blacks, highest in the South, lowest in the Northeast, and higher for high-income than for low-income households. The risk of death from homicide by a gun varies by age, race, and gender; young Black males are at highest risk. Approximately one-third of all privately owned firearms in this country are handguns; the remaining two-thirds are long guns of various types. Handguns are the homicide weapon of choice. In gun homicides for which the type of weapon is known, handguns account for nearly 80%. When compared with injuries from other weapons, firearm injuries are the most likely to be lethal. The case fatality rate—the fraction of injuries that lead to death—is two to five times greater for guns than for knives, the next most lethal weapon. An estimated 12.2% of gun attacks are fatal. The illegal market is an important source of firearms; it is estimated that only one firearm in six used in crime is legally obtained (Reiss & Roth, 1993, pp. 266–280).

The concern of this volume is mostly with primary homicides, those involving long-term intimate relationships. Such incidents occur usually in a private residence, and when a gun is used it is virtually always one kept in the home for personal protection. For that reason, a particularly pertinent question relates to the efficacy of keeping a firearm in the home. Does it enhance household safety? Arthur Kelermann and associates (1993) examined that question and concluded that the practice of keeping firearms in the home for the purpose of safety is counterproductive. Under current conditions, a gun kept in the home is far more likely to be involved in the death of a household member than it is to be used in self-defense against an intruder. One suggestion posed by this finding is that removal of firearms from the home through legislative coercion would reduce domestic homicide.

Legislated gun control as a means of homicide prevention is under debate, and evaluation research is limited, with mostly inconclusive findings. Two thousand disparate federal, state, and local laws focus on a variety of control options ranging from the elimination of all handguns from circulation to prohibition of use by certain categories such as youth, felons, or the mentally ill (Wright, Rossi, & Daly, 1983). Some laws restrict gun ownership, while others restrict carrying but not owning, and still others are concerned with the use of guns for criminal means. Reviews of evidence (Wright, Rossi, & Daly, 1983; Wright & Rossi, 1985; Kleck, 1991) conclude that lack of uniform legislation across jurisdictions weakens the violence reduction impact of what might otherwise prove to be effective legislation. For example, the strict laws of New York City and Washington, D.C. are rendered impotent by the fact that citizens can avoid restraints by simply stepping over into an adjacent jurisdiction (Wright & Rossi, 1985).

There are interventive alternatives to legislated gun control. Technological and public education interventive strategies have been employed to reduce the fatality associated with guns stored in the home for the purpose of self-defense. Development of such strategies suggests the belief that guns need not necessarily be removed from the home, but instead can be altered technologically to enhance safety in storage and usage, and that owners can be educated in ways of firearm use and safety. These nonlegislated control alternatives are appealing in light of the facts that most guns used in crime are illegally obtained (suggesting that legislative intervention would be ineffective anyway), and that many, if not most, primary homicides are not rationally intended to be lethal (suggesting that devices such as triggerlocks could save lives).

In their comprehensive literature review of firearm violence and preventive interventions to reduce it (including legislated,

technological, and public education-oriented), and e\
of those interventions, Albert Reiss and Jeffrey R\
pp. 255–287) conclude that evaluation results of most \
few control strategies that have been tested are inconcl\
three types of strategies—legislated, technological, and \
education-oriented—hold promise as the public health con.
nity joins forces with the criminal justice system to reduce fl.
arm-induced homicide through these means of primary prevention.

A third homicide risk factor that becomes apparent with this
Detroit research and that is recognized consistently in the literature, is alcohol consumption. Studies demonstrate a persistent
association across all types of homicide except that perpetrated
by children (Rosenberg & Mercy, 1991, p. 27). About half of offenders and victims had been drinking at the time of the offense
(The National Committee for Injury Prevention and Control,
1989, p. 197; Reiss & Roth, 1993, p. 184). The four profiles included in this volume that report information on alcohol consumption (Chapters 1, 2, 3, & 4) conform to this previously established pattern.

Evidence indicates no direct causal relationship between
alcohol consumption and violence, including homicide, "but
rather a network of interacting processes and feedback loops"
(Reiss & Roth, 1993, p. 183). The authors of a major literature
review conclude: "While research has shown that alcohol is involved in substantial proportions of . . . violent events, understanding of the ways in which alcohol consumption contributes
to violence remains very limited" (Mercy, Davidson, Goodman,
& Rosenberg, 1986). The message of consensus here is that it is
not the chemical property of alcohol that causes people to be
violent, and as yet no acceptable explanation for the relationship
has surfaced.

Actually, there is one viable and intuitively appealing set of
explanatory evidence that is cited only in passing in the literature and accorded little weight in the theoretical scheme of things
(Reiss & Roth, 1993, pp. 198–200). The theory springs from cross-
cultural observations and studies of alcohol-related social expec-

tation (Gelles, 1993). Cross-cultural studies demonstrate that behavioral response to alcohol consumption is culture-bound: countries populated by Europeans and their descendants show positive associations between alcohol use and violence, but non-European cultures show no such consistent relationship. Furthermore, there is a general tendency among the various non-European cultures to conform to a variety of alcohol-related social expectations. For example, intoxicated Navajo fight almost exclusively with kin. And Plains Native-American men are expected to fight when intoxicated only when they are young (Heath, 1983). Craig MacAndrew and Robert Edgerton (1969) argue that drunken comportment is situation-specific and learned. In our society, as well as many others, people learn that they will not be held responsible for their behavior while intoxicated. Alcohol consumption provides a "time-out" from normal rules of behavior—an excuse for violence.

This cultural pattern explanation for the relationship between alcohol consumption and violence is incomplete, as indicated by behavioral differences across individuals and situations within a single culture. Yet it is persuasive in debunking the myth of the drunk and crazed murderer and the notion that curing the alcohol problem will eliminate violent behavior. Unfortunately, health practitioners and clinicians erroneously raise hopes that treatment of the abuse is simultaneously treatment for violence. A primary prevention strategy for alcohol-related homicide based on the cultural pattern explanation would be the launching of a public awareness campaign relaying the message that "alcohol is just an excuse."

INTERVENTIONS TO PREVENT HOMICIDE

The public health approach has come to represent a unified framework for developing relevant information and transforming it into preventive action. While all levels of prevention—primary, secondary, and tertiary—apply, primary prevention, with its focus on broad social change, is the central strategy, followed by secondary prevention. The intention is to intervene early in the developmental trajectory of the problem—to "nip it in the bud" if possible. Public health aims to prevent disease and injury through any and all means available. The focus is on three strategies: 1) altering individual knowledge, skills, and attitudes; 2) altering the social environment; and 3) altering the physical environment (Mercy, Rosenberg, Powell, Broome, & Roper, 1993, p. 14). Perhaps the most visible of public health efforts conform to the first strategy. In its attempt to shape beliefs, attitudes, and ultimately behavior, public health prefers education to coercive legal approaches. This is because experience has shown that when certain forms of conduct are criminalized, the behavior is driven underground, rendering the epidemics harder, rather than easier, to control (Moore, forthcoming). While primary prevention is the strategy of choice of public health, all too often desired changes are too slow in coming and must be supplemented with secondary and tertiary strategies.

Beyond the interventions suggested above relating to poverty, firearm abuse, and alcohol consumption, are numerous others that have been offered by a variety of sources, including the National Commission on Violence (Mulvihill & Tumin, 1969), the Attorney General's Task Force on Family Violence (1984), *Injury Prevention: Meeting the Challenge* (National Committee for Injury Prevention and Control, 1989), the National Research Council's Panel on Understanding and Control of Violent Behavior (Reiss & Roth, 1993), *Violence in America: A Public Health Approach* (Rosenberg & Fenley, 1991) and James Mercy and colleagues' comprehensive essay, "Public Health Policy for Preventing Violence" (1993). These reports should be reviewed by those who seek detailed familiarity with specific preventive interventions. What follows is a selection of proposed interventions considered as part of a broad-based, sustained strategy to prevent violence in general and homicide in particular. The selections are relevant to the epidemiologic studies constituting this volume. Risk factors differentating fatal from nonfatal violence against spouses and children remain unknown (though an instrument designed to detect that difference in spouses is in development [Campbell, 1992b]), so prevention strategies are the same. The prevention approaches offered here for spouse and child abuse therefore apply to homicide against spouses, and in early childhood, respectively.

Decrease the Cultural Acceptance of Violence

In our nation, brutal violence is tolerated toward many minorities, including children, women, homosexuals, African Americans, and incarcerated felons. Acceptance of violence is demonstrated through policies and laws allowing corporal and capital punishment and through patronage of screen violence. Most of us have seen the figures relating to national television-viewing habits and T.V. violence: children aged 2 to 11 log an average of 28 hours per week, which means that at the end of elementary school they have seen more than five thousand murders. Research is convincing that T.V. is a cause of violence in general and homicide in particular (Barry, 1993, p. 40). The public needs to be informed of this causal connection, and persuaded to avoid violent programming. The public also needs to be persuaded to reject violence in its many other forms.

Reduce Gender Inequality

The hierarchically gendered nature of our social structure is conducive to violence against women in general, and to the battering of women that sometimes results in intimate-partner homicides against both wives and husbands. Women can become held captive in intimate relationships with controlling and violent men because norms dictate that women "need" and should personally serve men—and the entire socioeconomic order operates to maintain women's subordination to men—low pay and lack of good and affordable day care, effective child support enforcement policy, and parental leave policy, regardless of business size. Only when our world is free of gender inequality, when women and men can enjoy relationships of mutual respect, will gendered violence and deaths stop.

Install Programs in Medical Agencies Designed to Identify, Treat, Educate, and Support Abuse Victims

Nearly 20% of women presenting with physical injuries at hospitals have been abused. Also, an estimated 17% of women who have been battered have used emergency medical services. The health professional is often the first or only person to whom a battered woman turns, if only because her problems require medical attention. These facts indicate that medical agencies are perhaps *the* crucial point in the initial identification, treatment, and prevention of abuse (Stark & Flitcraft, 1992, p. 1040). In 1992, the American Medical Association published guidelines to aid in the identification of wife abuse in the emergency room, and the Division on Women of the State of New Jersey's Department of Community Affairs has published a list of questions designed to elicit critical information from battered women about their abuse (Perrone, 1992, p. 160). So the need has been established and the ideological backing and the tools are in place. Since 1986 Children's Hospital in Boston has been pioneering an abuse intervention program, Advocacy for Women and Kids in Emergencies (AWAKE), which is designed to accommodate both women and children.

Improve Police and Community Response to Battering

Police, along with medical agencies, occupy the front lines of refuge for battered women and children. Agency response is critical in light of the fact that it is often in its hands alone that victims will place trust—a daunting responsibility. One of the few violence intervention strategies that have been evaluated systematically is police intervention in misdemeanor spouse assault. The National Institute of Justice sponsored a program of randomized field experiments and replications to test the relative effectiveness of different forms of police intervention in preventing recurrences of spouse assault—the Minneapolis Domestic Violence Experiment. The randomized treatments included arrest of the offending spouse, police counseling of both parties, and temporary separation of the assailant. Lawrence Sherman and Richard Berk (1984) concluded that arrest was the most effective of the three police responses. To test the validity of that finding, replications were conducted in six U.S. locations. Those experiments replicated the arrest treatment, but tested other police interventions in each location.

Scrutiny of available information on the subject demonstrates that, as with violence outside the family, arrest is not usually a deterrent to repeated wife abuse. At this point we know of no such deterrent. Yet widespread presumptive and mandatory arrest policy persist in this country. Policy mandating arrest is not defensible because under some conditions arrest may well increase the incidence of abuse (Sherman, 1992), and it is costly. Mechanistic arrest patronizes battered women. Instead, victims should be allowed control over the outcome of police intervention (Buzawa & Buzawa, 1993). Ending the battering permanently and safely, whether by exit or desistance, is usually a multistage process, one heavily encumbered with fits, starts, and reversals. Probably the victim knows better than anyone else where she stands in that process and what kind of help she needs from her community. We should move forward identifying and developing the support systems required by these women to do what they decide that they must do as they pursue their own personal journey to liberation.

Increase Education for Family Life, Family Planning, and Child Rearing

Education in these areas holds promise for abating family stress and violence. Family planning information and services decrease the incidence of unwanted and unexpected children born into families with neither the inclination nor the resources to nurture and support these children. Parent- and family-life education programs designed to serve all potential parents are desirable because they eliminate the need to identify at-risk families. Such curricula should include preventive education as well as instruction relating to the reporting of abuse and should be integrated into grades K–12 of the public school system. Bringing these programs into the schools is a good idea because most parents at risk for child abuse are reluctant to attend parent-group meetings (Olds & Henderson, 1989, p. 724). Curtailing violence in the home will save lives there and, by reducing the amount of violence learned, also prevent deaths perpetrated against acquaintances and strangers. Family education about developmental difficulties would help parents identify those difficulties and seek appropriate treatments for children with special needs (Rosenberg & Mercy, 1991, pp. 41–42).

Provide Nurse Home Visitation

Home visiting programs for infants and preschoolers of at-risk parents are desirable as preventive intervention for one of the same reasons that public school programs serve well in that capacity: they do not require these parents to come to meetings. National programs of this kind exist in the United Kingdom and some European countries. Only one methodologically sound experiment involving a visiting nurse program in the U.S. has been reported (Reiss & Roth, 1993, p. 243). Olds and his colleagues randomly assigned 400 first-time mothers to three treatment groups with incrementally increasing services and one control group (Olds & Henderson, 1989). The third treatment group received nurse home visitation for the longer time, through the child's first two years of life. While all results were in the expected direction, the highest risk mothers—poor, unmarried teenagers—who received the most comprehensive treatment demonstrated statistically significantly less child abuse and neglect than the controls. Other positive outcomes were identified as well. Nurse home visitation is a primary prevention strategy that also provides a basis for secondary and tertiary intervention.

MOVING FORWARD

Consistent with the public health vision, an increasing number of localities, inner-city schools and hospitals, community mental health centers and public health professional associations are establishing violence prevention programs. A few of these programs have been deemed effective through rigorous long-term evaluations. Others, involving such strategies as public awareness campaigns, emergency room screening for persons at risk of future involvement in violent incidents, and peer and family violence curricula for inner-city schools, have shown promising preliminary outcomes (Oliver, 1989, p. 269). Still, the efficacy of most active-prevention programs remains undetermined. We know more about risk groups and risk factors than we do about which prevention programs work and why. In the years directly before us we look forward to evaluation research shepherding us into a less violent world.

To interrupt the cycle of violence that is pulverizing the social fabric of our nation will require heartfelt commitment to diversity and collaboration across the social, behavioral, and biological sciences, evaluation research, and policy analysis. It will require an alliance between criminal justice and public health. Programs proven effective at local, state, and regional levels will need to be synthesized in meaningful ways and implemented, or at least supported, at the national level. Only the federal government has enough resources to make a national impact; federal funding must be used to leverage private and state/local initiatives.

But can our nation afford to stop the violence? Yes. In fact we can't afford not to. We know enough to begin. The National Committee for Injury Prevention and Control (1989, p. 1) states:

A comprehensive view of the state of the art in injury prevention demonstrates that, while questions remain, we already know enough to act. Indeed, if the interventions recommended in this book were put into general practice, the result would be a dramatic saving in lives, health, and resources. Moreover, it is only by acting and evaluating the impact of such actions that we will learn more. For both reasons, then—to save lives and to learn more about saving lives—injury prevention programs must be undertaken now.

Violence prevention will require up-front money, but we can find it. It is a matter of priority and political will.

Consider the low-income housing problem as an example. Given that the number of American prison cells more than doubled during the 1980s, while funding for housing for the poor was cut by more than half, and given that the cost of a new prison cell in New York was about the average cost of a new home purchased in the the U.S. nationally ($30,000), in some ways prison became the American low-income housing policy of choice of the 1980s (Curtis, 1992, p. 4). We overincarcerate, and incarceration does not reduce crime.

Another example: although the cold war is over, we continue to spend $813 million per day on military—$25 billion more than during the average year of the cold war. Meanwhile, we claim that we are too poor to invest $23 million per day to assure every American child a healthy start, including prenatal care, immunization, preventive health checkups, and treatment (*The State of America's Children 1992*, 1992, p. xii). America can do what America wants to do with its money.

Our investment in violence prevention will pay off. The cost of violence in dollars defies estimates (Meyer, 1992, p. 155; Thomas, 1994). "It is cheaper to send a youngster to Yale than jail," says Lynn Curtis, President of the Milton S. Eisenhower Foundation (*No Quick Fix*, 1992). And the costs in human misery are incomprehensible. For the men, women, and children who live in America—for the nation as a whole—failure to act means that the years to come will be less safe, less caring, less free.

IN CLOSING

This book closes with the collective voice of Surgeon General Antonia Novello, Consultant to Surgeon General John Shosky, and Robert Froehke of the Division of Epidemiology, Michigan State Department of Public Health (1992, p. 21). The wisdom and compassion captured in their words provide a powerful source of direction in our search for relief from the violence and killing around us. Their message, representative of the public health agenda, is painfully clear. No one says it better:

> Violence can not be curbed by talking alone. If we are to succeed in stemming the epidemic of violence, we must first address the social, economic, and behavioral causes of violence. We must try to improve living conditions for millions of Americans. We must try to provide the economic and educational opportunities for our youth that racism and poverty destroy. Health care must become affordable and accessible for all Americans. We must help the educational system to instill the values that hold our society together. We must maintain and strengthen our families.
>
> . . . we need to change the way we view each other and treat each other. We must offer a strong sense of community, not a feeling of alienation. We must encourage recognition of the importance of each individual and teach the politics of inclusion, not exclusion. We must offer hope and take the necessary steps to make that hope a reality.

References

Adelson, L. (1961, June). Slaughter of innocents: A study of forty-six homicides in which the victims were children. *The New England Journal of Medicine, 264* (26), 1345–1349.

Adelson, L. (1973). The battering child. *Criminologist, 8,* 26–33.

Adler, E. S. (1981). The underside of married life: Power, influence, and violence. In L. H. Bowker (Ed.), *Women and crime in America* (pp. 300–319). New York: Macmillan.

Allen, N. H. (1980). *Homicide: Perspectives on prevention.* New York: Human Science Press.

Anthony, E. J., & Rizzo, A. (1973). Adolescent girls who kill or try to kill their fathers. In A. E. James & C. Koupernick (Eds.), *The child in his family: The impact of disease and death* (pp. 333–350). New York: John Wiley.

Attorney General's Task Force on Family Violence. (1984). Final Report, Washington, DC.

Bachand, D. (1983, August). *The elderly offender: A question of leniency in criminal processing.* Paper presented at the annual meeting of the American Sociological Association, Detroit, MI.

Barry, D. (1993). Screen violence: It's killing us. *Harvard Magazine, 96*(2), 38–43.

Bensing, R. C., Schroeder, O., Jr., & Jackson, P. B. (1960). *Homicide in an urban community.* Springfield, IL: Charles C. Thomas.

Block, C. R. (1985). *Lethal violence in Chicago over seventeen years: Homicides known to police, 1965–1981.* Chicago: Illinois Criminal Justice Information Authority.

Block, K. J. (1990). Age-related correlates of criminal homicides committed by women: A study of Baltimore. *Journal of Crime and Justice, 13*(1), 42–65.

Block, R. (1976). Homicide in Chicago: A nine-year study (1965–1973). *Journal of Criminal Law and Criminology, 66*, 496–510.

Block, R. (1979). Community, environment, and violent crime. *Criminology, 17*(1), 46–57.

Block, C. R., & Block, R. (1993). *Street gang crime in Chicago* (NCJ 144782). U.S. Department of Justice, Office of Justice Programs, National Institute of Justice (Research in Brief). Washington, DC: U.S. Government Printing Office.

Browne, A. (1986). Assault and homicide at home: When battered women kill. In M. J. Saks & L. Saxe (Eds.), *Advances in applied social psychology, Vol. 3.* (pp. 1–37). Durham, NC: Family Research Laboratory, University of New Hampshire.

Browne, A. (1987). *When battered women kill.* New York: Free Press.

Browne, A. (1988). Family homicide: When victimized women kill. In V. Van Hasselt, R. L. Morrison, A. S. Bellack, & M. Herson (Eds.), *Handbook of Family Violence* (pp. 271–289). New York: Plenum.

Browne, A. (1989). Resource availability for women at risk and partner homicide. *Law and Society Review, 23*, 75–94.

Browne, A., & Williams, K. R. (1993). Gender, intimacy, and lethal violence: Trends from 1976 through 1987. *Gender and Society, 7*(1), 78–98.

Brownstein, H. H., Spunt, B. J., Crimmins, S., Goldstein, P. J. & Langley, S. (1994). Changing patterns of lethal violence by women: A research note. *Women & Criminal Justice, 5*(2), 99–118.

Brownstein, H. H., Spunt, B. J., Crimmins, S., & Langley, S. (1993). *Political economy and homicide by women.* Paper presented at the annual meeting of the American Society of Criminology, Phoenix.

Bunyak, J. R. (1986). Battered women who kill: Civil liability and the admissibility of battered woman's syndrome testimony. *Law and Inequality, IV*(3), 606–636.

Buzawa, E. S., & Buzawa, C. G. (1993). The scientific evidence is not conclusive: Arrest is no panacea. In R. J. Gelles & D. R. Loseke (Eds.), *Current controversies in family violence.* Newbury Park, CA: Sage Publications.

Campbell, J. C. (1992a). "If I can't have you, no one can": Power and control in homicide of female partners. In J. Radford & D. E. H.

Russell (Eds.), *Femicide: The politics of women killing*. New York: Twayne Publishers.

Campbell, J. C. (1992b). The danger assessment instrument: Risk factors of homicide of and by battered women. In C. R. Block & R. L. Block (Eds.), *Questions and answers in lethal and non-lethal violence. Proceedings of the first annual workshop of the Homicide Working Group.* Ann Arbor, MI, June 14–16). Washington, DC: U.S. Department of Justice, Office of Justice Programs, National Institutes of Justice (NCJ 142058).

Carlson, N. A. (1974, November 5). *Trends in criminal justice.* Paper presented to a luncheon meeting of the Springfield, Missouri Rotary Club.

Cazenave, N. A., & Zahn, M. A. (1992). Women, murder, and male domination: Police reports of domestic violence in Chicago and Philadelphia. In E. C. Viano (Ed.), *Intimate violence: Interdisciplinary perspectives.* Washington, DC: Hemisphere Publishing Corporation.

Cheatwood, D., & Block, K. J. (1990). Youth and homicide: An investigation of the age factor in criminal homicide. *Justice Quarterly, 7*(2), 265–292.

Child homicide—United States (1982, June 11). *MMWR, 31,* 292–294.

Christoffel, K. K. (1988). Child homicide in the United States: The road to prevention. In G. T. Hotaling, D. Finkelhor, J. T. Kirkpatrick, & M. A. Straus (Eds.), *Coping with family violence: Research and policy perspectives* (pp. 310–316). Newbury Park, CA: Sage.

Christoffel, K. K. (1990). Violent death and injury in U.S. children and adolescents. *American Journal of Diseases of Children, 144,* 697–706.

Christoffel, K. K., & Liu, K. (1983). Homicide death rates in childhood in 23 developed countries: U.S. rates atypically high. *Child Abuse and Neglect, 7,* 339–345.

Cohen, L. E., & Felson, M. (1979). Social change and crime rate trends: A routine activity approach. *American Sociological Review, 44,* 588–608.

Collins, J. J. (1981). *Drinking and crime: Perspectives on the relationships between alcohol consumption and criminal behavior.* New York: Guilford Press.

Conley, C. H., Kelly, P., Mohanna, & Warner, L. (1993). *Street Gangs: Current Knowledges and Strategies* (NCJ 143290). U.S. Department of Justice, Office of Justice Programs, National Institute of Justice (Issues and Practices). Washington, DC: U.S. Government Printing Office.

Cornell, D. G. (1989). Causes of juvenile homicide: A review of literature. In E. P. Benedek & D. G. Cornell (Eds.), *Juvenile homicide*. Washington, DC: American Psychiatric Press.

Cornell, D. G., Benedek, E. P., & Benedek, D. M. (1987). Characteristics of adolescents charged with homicide: Review of 72 cases. *Behavioral Sciences and the Law, 5*(1), 11–23.

Covey, H. C., Menard, S., & Fanzese, R. J. (1992). *Juvenile Gangs*. Springfield, IL: Charles C. Thomas.

Crimmins, S. (1993). Parricide vs. suicide: The dilemma of them or me. In A. V. Wilson (Ed.), *Homicide: The victim/offender connection*. Cincinnati, OH: Anderson Publishing Company.

Crimmins, S., Langley, S., Spunt, B. J., Brownstein, H. H., Cancel, E., Curry, P., Miller, T., & Sherman, E. (1993, November). *Convicted women who kill children: Preliminary research findings in New York State*. Paper presented at the annual meeting of the American Society of Criminology, Phoenix.

Cross, C. (July, 1986). Media Relations Manager, Michigan Bell Telephone Company, Detroit Michigan. (Telephone communication).

Curry, G. D., & Spergel, I. (1988). Gang homicide, delinquency and community. *Criminology, 26*(3), 381–405.

Curtis, L. A. (1974). *Criminal violence*. Lexington, MA: Lexington Books.

Curtis, L. A. (1992). Lord, how dare we celebrate? *Future Choices, 3*(3), 4.

Cutshall, C., & Adams, K. (1983). Responding to older shoplifters: Age selectivity in the processing of shoplifters. *Criminal Justice Review, 8*(2), 1–8.

Daly, M., & Wilson, M. (1987). Children as homicide victims. In R. J. Gelles & J. B. Lancaster (Eds.), *Child abuse and neglect: Biosocial dimensions* (pp. 201–214). New York: Aldine de Gruyter.

Daly, M., & Wilson, M. (1988). *Homicide*. New York: Aldine de Gruyter.

Daly, M., & Wilson, M. (1990). Killing the competition: Female/female and male/male homicide. *Human Nature, 1*(1), 81–107.

Dickens, B. M. (1969, September). Shops, shoplifting, and law enforcement. *Criminal Law Review*, 464–472.

Elliott, D. S. (1989). Criminal justice procedures in family violence crimes. In L. Ohlin & M. Tonry (Eds.), *Family violence* (pp. 427–480). Chicago: The University of Chicago Press.

Elliott, F. A. (1988). Neurological factors. In V. B. Van Hasselt, R. L.

Morrison, A. S. Bellack, & M. Herson (Eds.), *Handbook of family violence*. New York: Plenum Press.

Ewing, C. P. (1990). *When children kill: The dynamics of juvenile homicide*. New York: Free Press.

Fagan, J., Piper, E., & Moore, M. (1985, November). *Violent delinquents and urban youth: Correlates of survival and avoidance*. Paper presented at the annual meeting of the American Society of Criminology, San Diego, CA.

Fenstermaker, S., Berk, R. A., Loseke, D. R., & Rauma, D. (1983). Mutual combat and other family violence myths. In D. Finkelhor, R. J. Gelles, G. T. Hotaling, & M. A. Straus (Eds.), *The dark side of families: Current family violence research*. Beverly Hills, CA: Sage Publications.

Feinberg, G., & McGriff, D. M. (1986). *Elderly defendants: Protected or persecuted by the court system?* Paper presented at the annual meeting of the American Society of Criminology, Atlanta.

Felson, R. B., & Steadman, H. J. (1983). Situational factors in disputes leading to criminal violence. *Criminology, 21*, 59–74.

Fiala, R., & Lafree, G. (1988). Crossnational determinants of child homicide. *American Sociological Review, 53*, 432–445.

Foege, W. (1991). Preface. In M. L. Rosenberg & M. A. Fenley (Eds.), *Violence in America: A public health approach*. New York: Oxford University Press.

Frieze, I. H., & Browne, A. (1989). Violence in marriage. In L. Ohlin & M. Tonry (Eds.), *Family Violence* (pp. 163–218). Chicago: The University of Chicago Press.

Gardiner, M. (1976). *The deadly innocents: Portraits of children who kill*. New York: Basic Books.

Gartner, R. (1991). Family structure, welfare spending, and child homicide in developed democracies. *Journal of Marriage and the Family, 53*, 321–240.

Gelles, R. J. (1993). Alcohol and other drugs are associated with violence—they are not its cause. In R. J. Gelles & D. R. Loseke (Eds.), *Current controversies in family violence*. Newbury Park, CA: Sage Publications.

Gelles, R. J., & Cornell, C. P. (1985). *Intimate violence in families*: Beverly Hills, CA: Sage Publications.

Gelles, R. J., & Straus, M. A. (1989). *Intimate violence: The causes and consequences of abuse in the American family*. New York: Simon and Schuster, Inc. (Touchstone).

Gibbons, D. C. (1973). *Society, crime, and criminal careers: An Introduction to criminology* (2nd ed.). Englewood Cliffs, NJ: Prentice Hall.

Gilbert, E. (1992). *Violence in the family: Elderly homicide*. Paper presented at the annual meeting of the Academy of Criminal Justice Sciences, Pittsburgh, PA.

Gillespie, C. K. (1989). *Justifiable Homicide: Battered women, self-defense and the law*. Columbus: Ohio State University Press.

Gilligan, J. F. (1991). *The interpretation of violence: From homicide to genocide. Part II, Shame and humiliation: The emotions of individual and collective violence*. Cambridge, MA: 1991 Erikson Lectures, sponsored by the Erik and Joan Erikson Center, May 23. (Contact James F. Gilligan, Suite 2-F, 1010 Memorial Drive, Cambridge, MA, 02138).

Godwin, J. (1978). *The ways we kill each other*. New York: Ballantine.

Goetting, A. (1987). Homicidal wives: A profile. *Journal of Family Issues 8*, 332–341.

Goetting, A. (1988a). Patterns of homicide among women. *Journal of Interpersonal Violence, 3*, 3–19.

Goetting, A. (1988b). When females kill one another: The exceptional case. *Criminal Justice and Behavior, 15*, 179–189.

Goetting, A. (1988c). When parents kill their young children: Detroit 1982–86. *Journal of Family Violence, 3*, 339–346.

Goetting, A. (1989). Patterns of homicide among children. *Criminal Justice and Behavior, 16*, 63–80.

Goetting, A. (1992). Patterns of homicide among the elderly. *Violence and Victims, 7*, 203–215.

Goetting, A. (1994). Do Americans really like children? *The Journal of Primary Prevention, 15*(1), 81–92.

Griffin, E. E. H., & Bell, C. C. (1989). Recent trends in suicide and homicide among Blacks. *Journal of the American Medical Association, 262*(16), 2265–2269.

Gruhl, J., Welch, S., & Spohn, C. (1984). Women as criminal defendants: A test for paternalism. *Western Political Quarterly, 37*, 456–467.

Hamparian, D. M., Davis, J. M., Jacobson, J. M., & McGraw, R. E. (1985). *The young criminal years of the violent few*. Washington, DC: U.S. Department of Justice, Office of Juvenile Justice and Delinquency Prevention, National Institute for Juvenile Justice and Delinquency Prevention.

Hamparian, D. M., Schuster, R., Dinitz, S., & Conrad, J. P. (1978). *The violent few: A study of dangerous juvenile offenders*. Lexington, MA: D. C. Heath.

Hartstone, E., & Hansen, K. V. (1984). The violent juvenile offender: An empirical portrait. In R. A. Mathias, P. DeMuro, & R. S. Allison (Eds.), *Violent juvenile offenders: An anthology* (pp. 83–112). San Francisco: National Council on Crime and Delinquency.

Heath, D. B. (1983). Alcohol and aggression: A "missing link" in worldwide perspective. In E. Gottheil, K. A. Druley, T. E. Skoloda, & H. M. Waxman (Eds.), *Alcohol, drug abuse and aggression*. Springfield, IL: Thomas.

Heide, K. M. (1986). A taxonomy of murder: Motivational dynamics behind the homicidal acts of adolescents. *Journal of Justice Issues, 1*, 3–9.

Heide, K. M. (1993a). Juvenile involvement in multiple offender and multiple victim parricides. *Journal of Police and Criminal Psychology, 9*(2), 53–64.

Heide, K. M. (1993b). Parents who get killed and children who kill them. *The Journal of Interpersonal Violence, 8*(4), 531–544.

Heide, K. M. (1994a). Evidence of child maltreatment among parricide offenders. *International Journal of Offender Therapy and Comparative Criminology, 37*(4), 151–162.

Heide, K. M. (1994b). Weapons used by juveniles and adults to kill parents. *Behavioral Sciences and the Law, 11*, 397–405.

Henton, J., Cate, R., Koval, J., Lloyd, S., & Christopher, S. (1983). Romance and violence in dating relationships. *Journal of Family Issues, 4*, 467–482.

Hotaling, G. T., & Sugarman, D. B. (1986). An analysis of risk markers on husband-to-wife violence: The current state of knowledge. *Violence and Victims, 1*(2), 101–124.

Huff, C. R. (Ed.). (1990). *Gangs in America*. Thousand Oaks, CA: Sage Publications.

Ingrassia, M., Annin, P., Biddle, N. A., & Miller, S. (1993, July 19). "Life means nothing." *Newsweek*, pp. 16–17.

Jason, J., Flock, M., & Tyler, C. W., Jr. (1983). Epidemiologic characteristics of primary homicides in the United States. *American Journal of Epidemiology, 117*(4), 419–428.

Jason, J., Strauss, L. T., & Tyler, C. W., Jr. (1983). A comparison of primary and secondary homicides in the United States. *American Journal of Epidemiology, 117*(3), 309–319.

Jenkins, E. J., & Bell, C. C. (1992). Adolescent violence: Can it be curbed? *Adolescent Medicine: State of the Art Reviews, 3*(1), 71–85.

Jerrone, J. (1992). "Red flags" offer clues in spotting domestic abuse. In *Violence*: A compendium from JAMA, American Medical News, and the specialty journals of the American Medical Association. Chicago: American Medical Association.

Jurik, N. C., & Gregware, P. (1992). A method for murder: The study of homicides by women. *Perspectives on Social Problems, 4*, 179–201.

Jurik, N. C., & Winn, R. (1990). Gender and homicide: A comparison of men and women who kill. *Violence and Victims, 5*(4), 227–242.

Kantor, G. K., Kaufman, G., & Straus, M. A., (1987, November). *Stopping the Violence: Battered Women, Police Utilization and Police Response*. Paper presented at the annual meeting of the Society of Criminology, Montreal, Canada.

Kelermann, A. L., Riverara, F. P., Rushforth, N. B., Banton, J. G., Reay, D. T., Francisco, J. T., Locci, A. B., Prodzinski, J., Hackman, B. B., & Somes, G. (1993). Gun ownership as a risk factor for homicide in the home. *The New England Journal of Medicine, 329* (15), 1084–1091.

Kempe, C. H., Silverman, F. N., Steele, B. F., Droegemueller, W., & Silver, H. K. (1962). The battered child syndrome. *Journal of the American Medical Association, 181*, 17–24.

Kennedy, D. B., & Homant, R. J., (1984). Battered women's evaluation of the police response. *Victimology, 9*, 174–179.

Kleck, G. (1991). *Point blank: Guns and violence in America*. New York: Aldine de Gruyter.

Koop, C. E., & Lundberg, G. D. (1992). Violence in America: A public health emergency. *Journal of the American Medical Association, 267*(22), 3075–3076.

Kratcoski, P. C. (1993). An analysis of cases involving elderly homicide victims and offenders. In E. C. Viano (Ed.), *Critical issues in victimology*. New York: Springer Publishing Company.

Kratcoski, P. C., & Walker, D. B. (1988). Homicide among the elderly: Analysis of the victim/assailant relationship. In B. McCarthy & R. Langworthy (Eds.), *Older offenders: Perspectives in criminology and criminal justice* (pp. 62–75). New York: Praeger.

La Grange, R. L., & Ferraro, K. F. (1989). Assessing age and gender differences in perceived risk and fear of crime. *Criminology, 27*, 697–719.

Langan, P. A., & Innes, C. A. (1986, Fall). Preventing domestic violence against women. Bulletin of the Criminal Justice Archive and Information Network, (CJAIN) Ann Arbor: University of Michigan Press.

Langley, S., Crimmins, S., Brownstein, H., Spunt, B., Cancel, E., Curry, P., Miller, T., & Sherman, S. (1993, November). *Typology of homicides committed by women: Beyond the battered woman syndrome*. Paper presented at the annual meeting of the American Society of Criminology, Phoenix.

Last, J. M. (Ed.). (1980). *Public health and preventive medicine* (11th Edition). New York: Appleton-Century-Crofts.

Last, J. M. (Ed.). (1986). *Public health and preventive medicine* (12th Edition). Norwalk, CT: Appleton and Lange.

Leborici, S. (1973). Children who torture and kill. In A. E. James & C. Koupernick (Eds.), *The child in his family: The impact of disease and death* (pp. 307–318). New York: John Wiley.

Leonard, K. E., & Jacob, T. (1988). Alcohol, alcoholism, and family violence. In V. B. van Hasselt, R. L. Morrison, & A. S. Bellack (Eds.), *Handbook of Family Violence* (pp. 383–406). New York: Plenum.

Lewis, D. O., Moy, E., Jackson, L. D., Aaronson, R., Restifo, S. S., & Simos, A. (1985). Biopsychosocial characteristics of children who later murder: A prospective study. *American Journal of Psychiatry, 142*, 1161–1167.

Lewis, D. O., Shanok, S. S., Grant, M., & Ritvo, E. (1983). Homicidally agressive young children: Neuropsychiatric and experimental correlates. *American Journal of Psychiatry, 140*, 148–153.

Loya, F., Mercy, J. A., Allen, N. H., Vargas, L. A., Smith, J. C., Goodman, R. A., & Rosenberg, M. L. (1985). *The epidemiology of homicide in the city of Los Angeles, 1970–79: A collaborative study by the University of California at Los Angeles and the Centers for Disease Control*. Atlanta, GA: U.S. Department of Health and Human Services, Public Health Service, Centers for Disease Control, Violence Epidemiology Branch.

Lindquist, J. H., & White, O. Z. (1987). Elderly felons: Disposition of arrests. In C. D. Chambers, J. H. Lindquist, & M. T. Harter (Eds.), *Elderly deviants and victims* (pp. 161–176). Athens, OH: Ohio University Press.

Luckenbill, D. F. (1977). Criminal homicide as a situated transaction. *Social Problems, 25*, 176–186.

MacAndrew, C., & Edgerton, R. B. (1969). *Drunken comportment: A social explanation*. Chicago: Aldine de Gruyter.

MacDonald, J. M. (1961). *The murderer and his victim*. Springfield, IL: Charles C. Thomas.

Mack, J. E., Scherl, D. J., & Macht, L. B. (1973). Children who kill their mothers. In A. E. James & C. Koupernick (Eds.), *The child in his family: The impact of disease and death* (pp. 319–332). New York: John Wiley.

MacNamara, D. E. J., & Sagarin, E. (1986). *Precocious criminals*. Unpublished book.

Mann, C. R. (1987). Black women who kill. In R. L. Hampton (Ed.), *Family violence in minority communities* (pp. 157–186). Lexington, MA: D. C. Heath.

Mann, C. R. (March, 1988) Getting even? Women who kill in domestic encounters. *Justice Quarterly, 5* (1), 33–51.

Mann, C. R. (1990). Black female homicide in the United States. *Journal of Interpersonal Violence, 5*(2), 176–201.

Mann, C. R. (1991). Black women who kill their loved ones. In R. L. Hampton (Ed.), *Black family violence: Current research and theory*. Lexington, MA: Lexington Books.

Mann, C. R. (1993a). Maternal filicide of preschoolers. In A. V. Wilson (Ed.), *Homicide: The victim/offender connection*. Cincinnati: Anderson Publishing Co.

Mann, C. R. (1993b). Sister against sister: Female intrasexual homicide. In C. C. Culliver (Ed.), *Female criminality: The state of the art*. New York: Garland Publishing, Inc.

Maxson, C. L., Gordon, M. A., and Klein, M. W. (1985). Differences between gang and nongang homicides. *Criminology, 23*(2), 209–222.

McClain, P. D. (1982). Black female homicide offenders: Are they from the same population? *Death Education, 6*, 265–278.

Mercy, J. A., Davidson, L. E., Goodman, R. A., & Rosenberg, M. L. (1986). *Alcohol and intentional violence: Implications for research and public policy*. Background paper for the National Institute on Alcohol Abuse and Alcoholism conference in Research Issues in the Prevention of Alcohol Related Injuries, Berkeley.

Mercy, J. A., & O'Carroll, P. W. (1988). New directions in violence prediction: The public health arena. *Violence and Victims, 3*(4), 285–301.

Mercy, J. A., Rosenberg, M. L., Powell, K. E., Broome, C. V., & Roper, W. L. (1993). Public health policy for preventing violence. *Health Affairs, 13*(4), 7–29.

Mercy, J. A., & Saltzman, L. E. (1989). Fatal violence among spouses in the United States. *American Journal of Public Health, 79*(5), 595–599.

Meyer, H. (1992). The billion-dollar epidemic. In *Violence*. A compendium from JAMA, American Medical News, and the specialty journals of the American Medical Association. Chicago: American Medical Association.

Michael, R., & Zumpe, D. (1986). An annual rhythm in the battering of women. *American Journal of Psychiatry, 143,* 637–640.

Mones, P. (1991). *When a child kills: Abused children who kill their parents.* New York: Pocket Books.

Moore, M. H., (Forthcoming). Preventing crime. *Crime and Justice: A Review of Research Volume 19.* Edited by Michael Tonry and David P. Farrington. Castine, ME: Castine Press.

Morash, M. (1986). Wife battering. *Criminal Justice Abstracts, 18,* 252–271.

Morganthau, T. (1989, March 13). Murder wave in the capital. *Newsweek,* pp. 16–19.

Morganthau, T. (1991, March 25). The war at home: How to battle crime. *Newsweek,* pp. 35, 36, 38.

Mulvihill, D. J., & Tumin, M. M. (Eds.). (1969). *Crimes of violence: A staff report submitted to the National Commission on the Causes and Prevention of Violence.* Washington, DC: U.S. Government Printing Office.

Munford, R. S., Kazeur, R. S., Feldman, R. A., & Stivers, R. R. (1976). Homicide trends in Atlanta. *Criminology, 14,* 213–232.

Muscat, J. E. (1988). Characteristics of childhood homicide in Ohio, 1974–84. *American Journal of Public Health, 78*(7), 822–824.

Myers, S. A. (1970). Maternal filicide. *American Journal of the Disabled Child. 120,* 534–536.

The National Committee for Injury Prevention and Control. (1989). *Injury prevention: Meeting the challenge.* New York: Oxford University Press.

Nevello, A. C., Shosky, J., & Froehke, R. (1992). From the Surgeon General: U.S. public health service. In *Violence* (A compendium from JAMA, American Medical News, and the specialty journals of the American Medical Association). Chicago: American Medical Association.

No quick fix. (1992). News conference, U.S. Senate, May 19. Washington, DC: The Milton S. Eisenhower Foundation.

Olds, D. L., & Henderson, C. R., Jr. (1989). The prevention of maltreatment. In D. Cicchetti & V. Carlson (Eds.), *Child maltreatment: Theory and research on the causes and consequences of child abuse and neglect*. New York: Cambridge University Press.

Oliver, W. (1989). Sexual conquest and patterns of Black-on-Black violence: A structural cultural perspective. *Violence and Victims, 4*(4), 257–273.

Pagelow, M. D. (1984). *Family violence*. New York: Praeger.

Parker, R. N. (1989). Poverty, subculture of violence, and type of homicide. *Social Forces, 67*(4), 983–1007.

Perrone, J. (1992). "Red flags" offer clues in spotting domestic abuse. In *Violence:* A compendium from JAMA, American Medical News, and the specialty journals of the American Medical Association. Chicago: American Medical Association.

Petrie, C., & Garner, J. (1990). Is violence preventable? In D. S. Besharov (Ed.), *Family violence: Research and public policy issues* (pp. 164–184). Washington, DC: The AEI Press.

Pettigrew, T. F., & Spier, R. B. (1962). The ecological structure of Negro homicide. *American Journal of Sociology, 67*, 621–629.

Plass, P. S., & Straus, M. A. (1987, July 6). *Intra-family homicide in the United States: Incidence, trends, and differences by region, race, and gender*. Paper presented at the Third National Family Violence Research Conference, University of New Hampshire, Durham.

Pokorney, A. D. (1965). A comparison of homicides in two cities. *Journal of Criminal Law, Criminology and Police Science, 56*, 479–487.

Prothrow-Stith, D. (1991). *Deadly consequences*. New York: Harper-Collins.

Rasche, C. (1988, March). *Characteristics of mate-homicides: A comparison to Wolfgang*. Paper presented at the annual meeting of the Academy of Criminal Justice Sciences, San Francisco.

Reiss, A. J., Jr. (1974). Discretionary justice in the United States. *International Journal of Criminology and Penology, 2*, 181–295.

Reiss, A. J., Jr., & Roth, J. A. (Eds.). (1993). *Understanding and preventing violence*. Washington, DC: National Academy Press.

Resnick, P. J. (1969). Child murder by parents: A psychiatric review of filicide. *American Journal of Psychiatry 26*, 325–334.

Resnick, P. J. (1970). Murder of the newborn: A psychiatric review of neonaticide. *American Journal of Psychiatry 126*, 1414–1420.

Riedel, M., Zahn, M. A., & Mock, L. F. (1985). *The nature and patterns of American homicide*. Washington, DC: U.S. Government Printing Office.

Robbins, C. A. (1990). Statement made as formal discussant of this paper at the 1990 annual meeting of the American Sociological Association, Washington, DC.

Rosenberg, M. L. (1988). Violence is a public health problem. *Transactions and Studies of the College of Physicians of Philadelphia, 10*(1–4), 147–168.

Rosenberg, M. L., & Fenley, M. A. (1991). *Violence in America: A public health approach*. New York: Oxford University Press.

Rosenberg, M. L., & Mercy, J. A. (1991). Assaultive violence. In M. L. Rosenberg & M. A. Finley (Eds.), *Violence in America: A public health approach*. New York: Oxford University Press.

Rosenfeld, R., & Decker, S. (1993). Where public health and law enforcement meet: Monitoring and preventing youth violence. *American Journal of Police, 12*(3), 11–57.

Rowley, J. C., Ewing, C. P., & Singer, S. I. (1987). Juvenile homicide: The need for an interdisciplinary approach. *Behavioral Sciences and the Law, 5*(1), 3–10.

Russell, D. H. (1979). Ingredients of juvenile murder. *International Journal of Offender Therapy and Comparative Criminology, 23*, 65–72.

Russell, D. H. (1982). *Rape in marriage*. New York: Macmillan.

Saving the Children (November, 1988). *Life*, p. 55.

Scott, P. D. (1973). Fatal battered baby cases. *Medical Science Law 13*, 197–206.

Sherman, L, & Berk, R. A. (1984). The specific deterrent effects of arrest for domestic assault. *American Sociological Review, 49*, 261–272.

Shichor, D., (1984). The extent and nature of lawbreaking by the elderly: A review of arrest statistics. In E. S. Newman, D. J. Newman, & M. L. Gewirtz (Eds.), *Elderly Criminals* (pp. 17–32). Cambridge, MA: Oelgeschlager, Gunn, and Hain, Publishers, Inc.

Shichor, D. (1985). Male–female differences in elderly arrests: An exploratory analysis. *Justice Quarterly 2*, 399–414.

Shichor, D., & Kobrin, S. (1978) Note: Criminal behavior among the elderly. *The Gerontologist, 19*(2), 213–218.

Silverman, I. J., Vega, M., & Danner, T. A. (1993). The female murderer. In A. V. Wilson (Ed.), *Homicide: The victim–offender connection*. Cincinnati, OH: Anderson Publishing Co.

Silverman, R. A., & Kennedy, L. W. (1988). Women who kill their children. *Violence and Victims, 3*(2), 113–127.

Silverman, R. A., & Kennedy, L. W. (1993). *Deadly deeds: Murder in Canada*. Scarborough, Ontario: Nelson Canada.

Smith, B. (1985, January 17). Assistant Administrator, Office of Wayne County Prosecuting Attorney. Personal Communication.

Smith, M. D., & Brewer, V. E. (1992). A sex-specific analysis of correlates of homicide victimization in United States cities. *Violence and Victims, 7*(4), 279–286.

Solway, K. S., Richardson, L., Hays, J. R., & Elion, V. H. (1981). Adolescent murderers: Literature review and preliminary research findings. In J. R. Hays, T. K. Roberts, & K. S. Solway (Eds.), *Violence and the violent individual* (pp. 193–209). New York: Spectrum.

Sorrels, J. M. (1977). Kids who kill. *Crime and Delinquency, 23,* 312–320.

Sorrels, J. M. (1980). What can be done about juvenile homicide? *Crime and Delinquency, 26,* 152–161.

SOSAD (1987, March 3). Detroiters will no longer stand for the slaughter of young people. *The Detroit Free Press*, p. 8A.

Stark, E., & Flitcraft, A. H. (1992). Spouse abuse. In J. M. Last & R. B. Wallace (Eds.), *Public health and preventive medicine* (13th ed., pp. 1040–1043). Norwalk, CT: Appleton & Lange.

The State of America's Children 1992 (1992). Washington, DC: The Children's Defense Fund.

Steinmetz, S. K., & Straus, M. A. (1974). *Violence in the family*. New York: Harper and Row.

Strang, H. (1993). *Child abuse homicides in Australia: Incidence, circumstances, prevention and control*. Paper presented at the Second World Conference on Injury Control, Atlanta.

Strasburg, P. A. (1978). *Violent delinquents*. New York: Monarch.

Straus, M. A. (1986). Domestic violence and homicide antecedents. *Bulletin of the New York Academy of Medicine, 62*(5), 446–465.

Straus, M. A., & Gelles, R. J. (Eds.). (1989). *Physical violence in American families: Risk factors and adaptations to violence in 8,145 families*. New Brunswick, NJ: Transaction.

Swigert, V. L., & Farrell, R. A. (1978). Patterns in criminal homicide: Theory and research. In P. Wickman & P. Whitten (Eds.), *Readings in criminology* (pp. 191–206). Lexington, MA: Health Lexington.

Thomas, P. (1994). A murder shows the crushing cost of U.S. crime. *International Herald Tribune, 6* July, p. 3.

Thompson, H. C., Bernstein, S. L., & Connelly, J. P. (1980). *Demographic and socioeconomic fact book on child health care*. Evanston, IL: American Academy of Pediatrics.

Tifft, L. L. (1993). Battering of women: The failure of intervention and the case for prevention. Boulder, CO: Westview Press.

Totman, J. (1978). *The murderess: A psychosocial study of criminal homicide*. San Francisco, CA: R and E Associates.

United States Department of Health, Education and Welfare. (1979). *The Surgeon General's Report on Health Promotion and Disease Prevention*. Washington, DC: U.S. Government Printing Office.

U.S. has highest rate of imprisonment in the world. (1991, January 7). *New York Times*.

U.S. Bureau of the Census (1982–83). *Current Population Survey*. Unpublished data.

U.S. Bureau of the Census (1983). *County and city data book*. Washington, DC: U.S. Government Printing Office.

U.S. Bureau of the Census (1982–86). *Statistical Abstract of the United States*. Unpublished data.

U.S. Bureau of the Census (1984–85). *Statistical abstract of the United States*. Unpublished data.

Viano, E. C. (1993). The child victim. In E. C. Viano (Ed.), *Critical issues in victimology*. New York: Springer Publishing Company.

von Hentig, H. (1948). *The criminal and his victim*. New Haven, CT: Yale University Press.

Voss, H. L., & Hepburn, J. R. (1968). Patterns in criminal homicide in Chicago. *Journal of Criminal Law, Criminology and Police Science, 59*, 499–508.

Walker, L. E. (1979). The battered woman. New York: Harper & Row.

Walker, L. E. (1989). *Terrifying love: Why battered women kill and how society responds*. New York: Harper & Row.

Weis, J. G. (1989). Family violence research methodology and design. In L. Ohlin, & M. Tonry (Eds.), *Family violence* (pp. 117–162). Chicago: The University of Chicago Press.

Weisheit, R. A. (1986). When mothers kill their children. *The Social Science Journal, 23*, 439–448.

Wilbanks, W. (1981, December 29). *Women as murder victims: An international perspective*. Paper presented at the Interdisciplinary Congress on Women, Haifa, Israel.

Wilbanks, W. (1982). Murdered women and women who murder. In N. H. Rafter & E. A. Stanko (Eds.), *Judge, lawyer, victim, thief:*

Women, gender roles and criminal justice (pp. 151–180). Boston: Northeastern University Press.

Wilbanks, W. (1983a). Female homicide offenders in the U.S. *International Journal of Women's Studies, 6*, 302–310.

Wilbanks, W. (1983b). The female homicide offender in Dade County, Florida. *Criminal Justice Review, 8*(2), 9–14.

Wilbanks, W. (1988). Are elderly felons treated more leniently by the criminal justice system? *International Journal of Aging and Human Development, 26*(4), 195–208.

Wilbanks, W., & Murphy, D. (1984). The elderly homicide offender. In E. S. Newman, D. J. Newman, & M. L. Gewritz (Eds.), *Elderly criminals* (pp. 79–91). Cambridge, MA: Oelgeschlager, Gunn, and Hain, Publishers, Inc.

Wilczynski, A., & Morris, A. (1993). Parents who kill their children. *Criminal Law Review, 18*, 31–36.

Wilson, M. I., & Daly, M. (1992). Who kills whom in spouse killings? On the exceptional sex ratio of spousal homicides in the United States. *Criminology, 30*(2), 189–215.

Winpisinger, K. A., Hopkins, R. S., Indian, R. W., & Hostetler, J. R. (1991). Risk factors for childhood homicides in Ohio: A birth certificate-based case-control study. *American Journal of Public Health, 81*(8), 1052–1054.

Wintemute, G. G., Teret, S., Kraus, J. F., Wright, M. A., & Bradfield, G. (1987). When children shoot children: Eighty-eight unintended deaths in California. *Journal of the American Medical Association, 257*(22), 3107–3109.

Wives face bigger risk in spouse killings. (1989, May 9). *Wall Street Journal*, p. B1.

Wolfgang, M. E. (1956) Husband-Wife Homicides. *Journal of Social Therapy, 2*, 263–271.

Wolfgang, M. E. (1958) *Patterns of criminal homicide*. Philadelphia: University of Pennsylvania Press.

Wolfgang, M. E., & Ferracuti, F. (1967). *The subculture of violence: Towards an integrated theory in criminology*. London: Tavistock.

Woodrum, E. (1990, March). *Intergender and interracial violence*. Paper presented at the annual meeting of the Southern Sociological Society, Louisville, KY.

Wright, J. D., & Rossi, P. H. (1985). *The armed criminal in America: A survey of incarcerated felons*. National Institute of Justice Research Report (July).

Wright, J. D., Rossi, P. H., & Daly, K. (1983). *Under the gun: Weapons, crime and violence in America*. Hawthorne, NY: Aldine Publishing Company.

Yllo, K., & Bograd, M. (Eds.). (1988). *Feminist perspectives on wife abuse*. Newbury Park, CA: Sage Publications.

Zahn, M. A. (n.d.). Violence prevention. Unpublished paper.

Zimring, F. E. (1968). Is gun control likely to reduce violent killings? *University of Chicago Law Review, 35*, 721–737.

Zimring, F. E. (1984). Youth homicide in New York: A preliminary analysis. *Journal of Legal Studies, 13*, 81–89.

Index

S *Springer Publishing Company*

EMPOWERING AND HEALING THE BATTERED WOMAN

A Model for Assessment and Intervention

Mary Ann Dutton, PhD

The book spells out in practical, concrete terms what it really means to place the pathology outside the battered woman. The novelty in this approach lies in the implications for practice: battered women are not "sick"—they are in a "sick" situation.

"...practical and comprehensive, an excellent guide for clinicians and other interveners.... integrates psychological theory with detailed information on the real-life dimensions of abuse and threat in interpersonal relationships. Her discussion of abused women's posttraumatic responses and the strategies for assessment that form a part of each chapter are particularly valuable."

—Angela Browne, PhD

Contents:

I. Conceptual Framework and Assessment: Women's Response to Battering: A Psychological Model • Understanding the Nature and Pattern of Abusive Behavior • Strategies to Escape, Avoid, and Survive Abuse • Psychological Effects of Abuse • Mediators of the Battered Woman's Response to Abuse

II. Intervention: Framework for Intervention with Victims and Survivors of Domestic Violence • Protective Interventions • Making Choices • Post-traumatic Therapy: Healing the Psychological Effects of Battering • Issues for the Professional Working with Abuse

1992   224pp   0-8261-7130-3   hardcover

536 Broadway, New York, NY 10012-3955 • (212) 431-4370 • Fax (212) 941-7842